I0172707

LIVE TO SERVE, LOVE TO SERVE

A Collection of Stories About Service, Leadership, and Changing the World

Written by members of Circle K International and the Kiwanis Family

Edited by Jeffrey G. Marsocci

For more information on Circle K, The Six Cents Initiative, or the Tomorrow Fund, please visit www.circlek.org.

To donate more money to the Six Cents Initiative, go to:

www.unicefusa.org/sixcentsonline

Cover by Amanda Badali of ajbadali Graphic Design, and cover design inspired by Charleston Dones, member of California State University-Sacramento Circle K who created the original Six Cents Initiative pin design for Circle K International.

For more information on Circle K, The Six Cents Initiative, or the Tomorrow Fund, please visit www.circlek.org..

Notes regarding this book

This book was created for two reasons. First and foremost, our world has a great need for young people to step forward and lead the way in making changes we desperately need. The stories contained in this book are touching, emotional, but most of all inspirational. Without action on your part to get involved and help change the world, then it is simply a nice book of stories. But if this book serves its primary purpose and pushes even one more person to get involved in their community, then it is a success.

The second, more direct benefit is that the profits from this book will go to the Six Cents Initiative through Circle K International (CKI) and UNICEF. CKI is a college-based service organization sponsored by Kiwanis to help promote clubs focused on service, leadership and fellowship. The Six Cents Initiative was a program developed by the 2006-2007 CKI President Alec Macauley, a then-senior from Duke University, and championed at the international level by CKI Service Project Chair Chad Taylor, a then-senior from Northern Kentucky University. They realized that six cents worth of rehydration salt crystals could save a child from death by dehydration. Therefore, all of the profits from this book will go to the Six Cents Initiative for as long as it is in existence, and any sales after that program is completed will go to a Circle K International-based scholarship fund or other designated charity.

As a final note, it is important to state clearly that while this book is being written based on submissions from members of Circle K International and the Kiwanis Family, this book is not being published by, is not sanctioned by, nor is the publisher officially affiliated with, Circle K International, Kiwanis International, or their subsidiaries or agents. This book is published by an independent publishing company, and all submissions reflect the stories and opinions of the respective authors and no one else.

For more information on Circle K, The Six Cents Initiative, or the Tomorrow Fund, please visit www.circlek.org.

For more information on Circle K, The Six Cents Initiative, or the Tomorrow Fund, please visit www.circlek.org..

About the Editor

Jeffrey G. Marsocci was born in Fort Worth, Texas, and raised in Lincoln, Rhode Island, where he graduated from Mount Saint Charles Academy High School. He received his Bachelor's degree in Business from Hofstra University, and two years later earned his law degree from the same university.

In 2004, he received a Certificate Degree in Non-Profit Management from Duke University, and has earned his Legal Master of Estate Preservation designation from the *Abts Institute for Estate Preservation*. Jeff also serves as a member of the Legal Council for The Estate Plan™, a nationally recognized estate preservation company headed by Henry W. Abts, III, trust guru and author of *The Living Trust*.

Jeff has led his own firm in Raleigh, North Carolina, since 1996, focusing on the areas of Wills, Trusts and Life & Estate Planning with a concentration in finding creative and impactful solutions to assist his clients in reaching their goals. He is also a founding member of The National Institute for Domestic Partner Estate Planning, and he frequently participates in programs to educate attorneys, financial advisors and accountants on estate planning issues.

Jeff and his wife Kathleen are active members of their community, working with youth leadership organizations throughout North Carolina and South Carolina. Jeff and Kathy also each received the President's Call to Service Award for performing more than 4,000 hours of service during their lifetimes.

For more information on Circle K, The Six Cents Initiative, or the Tomorrow Fund, please visit www.circlek.org.

For more information on Circle K, The Six Cents Initiative, or the Tomorrow Fund, please visit www.circlek.org..

This book is dedicated to those who realize they have the power and responsibility to change the world, and so they do... no matter their age, no matter their circumstances, and no matter how many times their elders tell them to leave well enough alone.

For more information on Circle K, The Six Cents Initiative, or the Tomorrow Fund,
please visit www.circlek.org..

Foreword

Each summer for the last fifty years, members of Circle K International, the world's premier collegiate service organization, have gathered in a major city for their annual convention. Drawing members from across the globe, this signature event is a unique opportunity for the exchange of ideas and information. During the late summer of 2006, the membership gathered in Boston, Massachusetts to perform service, share fellowship with one another, and elect the leaders who would guide the organization through the upcoming year. At that convention, important decisions were made, a diverse group of leaders was elected, and the unique journey of an idea for a charitable fundraising initiative began.

Throughout its history, Circle K International has made a tremendous impact on not only the campuses and communities where it is present, but also on the entire world through its fundraising efforts. Its small but devoted membership has consistently demonstrated an ability to raise money in unique and exciting ways for the betterment of the children of the world. Beginning in 1994, this fundraising potential was showcased through Circle K International's participation with the other branches of the Kiwanis Family in the fight to eradicate Iodine Deficiency Disorder (IDD). More recently, members helped Circle K International's Tomorrow Fund reach endowment through the "Shave The Wave" campaign spearheaded by 2004-2005 Circle K International President Troy C. Dibley. Each time a fundraising challenge was presented to Circle K International, its members rose to the challenge in order to help make the world a better place.

With this history of successful campaigns, and no organization-wide project underway, the time seemed perfect for the creation of a new fundraising initiative. Through many conversations with Kiwanis Family members from the Carolinas District and across the globe, 2006-2007 Circle K International President Alec Macaulay had seen the potential for a successful campaign, and pledged to the membership during his campaign that if elected, the creation of a fundraising initiative would be among his top priorities. His vision was to create a fundraiser that the entire organization could embrace, by working with one of Circle K International's partner organizations, tackling a quantifiable problem so that each dollar raised could make a measurable impact, and by finding a project that would align with the mission of the entire Kiwanis Family: Serving the Children of the World. Following the election and installation of the 2006-2007 Board of Trustees in Boston, work began on making this ambitious idea into a reality.

For more information on Circle K, The Six Cents Initiative, or the Tomorrow Fund, please visit www.circlek.org..

At first, the idea was received with only lukewarm enthusiasm by some. In retrospect, it seems perfectly logical that some would not immediately get behind the idea of creating a global project requiring an intricate partnership with another organization. Considering the substantial decisions facing the organization and its leaders in regards to the future direction of Circle K International, the thought of such an immense additional undertaking was perhaps daunting at best.

Thankfully, the idea had its passionate believers, and foremost among them was Trustee Chad Taylor. Appointed as the chair of the Service Committee, he was in an excellent position to have open dialogue with other organizations with which we held a partnership and to create directives toward the establishment of the fundraising initiative. By making work toward the initiative's creation a priority for the Service Committee, the first steps were taken toward the transformation of the project from an idea to a reality. In the midst of numerous other duties, the Service Committee set about laying the groundwork for the potential project.

Over many weeks and months, the work continued and the initiative began to take shape. Two of Circle K International's service partners, UNICEF and the March of Dimes, were asked to submit proposals for a potential fundraising partnership. We did our best to explain our vision for the initiative to them, but were a bit unsure of what types of opportunities we would be presented with. However, after receiving four remarkable proposals, each with its own unique way of making an impact on a global problem affecting children, it began to become increasingly clear that this would become a reality.

The proposals were received by leaders and membership alike with overwhelming support. Many who had previously been wary about the concept changed their minds and became fantastic supporters. The membership was asked for their input via an online poll on which proposal they most wanted to see set into motion, and after all the votes were counted, one was chosen.

Work began in earnest to gather information, create materials, and establish promotion for the new initiative in time for it's unveiling at the 2007 Circle K International Convention in Portland, Oregon. Utilizing the collective efforts of staff from UNICEF, Kiwanis International, and select devoted members of Circle K International, the new initiative began to take shape. Soon marketing materials were being created, forums and workshops were being planned to educate the membership, and a tremendous presentation was made to grandly introduce the new project to the membership. It is important to note that none of these things would have been possible without the tireless efforts of Kristi Burnham, our partner with UNICEF, Denise Lopez Domowicz, former Circle K International Director Casey Keller, and Elizabeth Warren. When convention began, the time had finally come. The idea that had blossomed into a dream was finally a reality for Circle K International and its members.

The new charitable fundraising project is now known as the Six Cents Initiative, which focuses on the worldwide problem of unclean and unsafe drinking water and the illness and death it causes among children. To those of us in industrialized nations, water is often and easily taken for granted as the most abundant resource on the planet. However for the over one billion people around the world who do not have access to safe drinking water, this problem is at the forefront of the fight for their lives and the lives of their children each and every day. Contaminated drinking water causes illness in millions of people each year, but among children, many of whom do not yet have strong immune systems, a problem as simple as diarrhea can threaten their life.

The Six Cents Initiative was created to help combat the rampant disease and death that is plaguing children around the world. For only six cents, a child can be given a packet of oral rehydration salts that will help combat dehydration and the diseases caused by unsafe water. This simple act is the namesake of this incredible project, because for that seemingly miniscule amount of money, we have the power to save the life of a child.

The members of Circle K International, past, present, and future, now have an opportunity to make a profound impact on their world through their involvement with the Six Cents Initiative. By raising money for this project, we have the power to save the lives of countless children around the world. The impact of our actions can and will be felt long after our actions themselves will have ended. Through even the simplest acts of charity, we can have a profound impact on the lives of people who we may never meet.

Circle K International has made a commitment to UNICEF to raise $500,000 through the Six Cents Initiative. This is as great a financial undertaking as Circle K International has had in its long and storied history. However, do not be daunted by the monumental task set before our organization. Circle K International has touched the lives of many people, not least of all its very own members. We have the capability, through our actions, to change the world for the better. There is no donation too small, no project too simple, and no person who is unable to have an impact. United behind our goal, there is nothing that we cannot accomplish.

For more information on Circle K, The Six Cents Initiative, or the Tomorrow Fund, please visit www.circlek.org.

We are proud to have been a part of the creation of the Six Cents Initiative, and we look forward to seeing the great work this project will continue to do for many years to come. Our service comes from a desire to help others we will never meet, change the lives of people we will never know, and to make the world a better place for all who come after us. Through our story, and the stories found in these pages, we hope to be able to pass that passion for service on to each of you.

In service, leadership, and fellowship,

Alec Macaulay, 2006-2007 Circle K International President
Chad Taylor, 2006-2007 Circle K International Trustee

For more information on Circle K, The Six Cents Initiative, or the Tomorrow Fund, please visit www.circlek.org.

For more information on Circle K, The Six Cents Initiative, or the Tomorrow Fund, please visit www.circlek.org..

TABLE OF CONTENTS

For more information on Circle K, The Six Cents Initiative, or the Tomorrow Fund, please visit www.circlek.org.

For more information on Circle K, The Six Cents Initiative, or the Tomorrow Fund,
please visit www.circlek.org..

Introduction

Throughout my adult life, I have had the privilege of serving others. While there are numerous ways people can serve, I have felt drawn to helping organizations become more effective, to helping their members become more effective leaders. From the time I was in college working on the weekly newspaper to the present working on leadership development with Circle K officers in the Carolinas, I wanted to help people become better at improving their communities.

I have also been blessed with wonderful teachers who stressed the value of writing effectively and writing well. From tenth and eleventh grade English with Sister Jackie Crepeau to writing books in my chosen profession of law, each step has prepared me for the next. The more I learned and practiced writing, the better I became not just in my own writing, but also in helping others write well.

In my experience, there are also no better stories than those that are true. I have seen none more passionate about life, more insistent in their beliefs, and more committed to improving their world than the current generation of college students who volunteer. Whether it's by building Habitat houses, working with kids in after school programs, or organizing blood drives, the college students of Circle K have been at the forefront of helping their communities. But each one started with their own story, their own moment of clarity of purpose that inspired them to move from being an occasional volunteer to joining a club focused on making the world a better place one child and one community at a time.

For more information on Circle K, The Six Cents Initiative, or the Tomorrow Fund, please visit www.circlek.org.

I now have the opportunity to utilize my own passion for writing to help these members of Circle K tell their stories. In the end, these will not be my stories, or even their stories. Instead, they will be stories that come from the heart, from the spirit that drives us to help others in need. Any story, no matter how personal, that has the power to inspire people to change the world really belongs to the world. And it is my hope that this book will touch something within your own heart and make you realize how much you can impact the world for the better.

For those who have already been touched by their own tale of service, you know what I'm talking about.

My own Circle K moment was not that long ago, although it was long past the time I could have considered myself a college student. Although I had been working with Circle K in one fashion or another for years, it was in the Spring of 2007 when I was running a training weekend for the newly elected Circle K club officers of North and South Carolina. We had spent a few hours getting to know each other through a series of activities, and then I introduced the officers to the elements of strategic planning, including creating a vision and mission statement for their club for the coming year. In brief, vision statements are simple one or two sentences that describe how an organization wishes to impact the world. Mission statements are another few sentences describing the main ways how an organization wishes to impact the world.

Before they started work on their own club vision and mission statements, I asked them to dream big and not feel confined to simple things that people expected them to do. I challenged them to find some big problems in their community that needed to be addressed, and then find ways to make those changes. Then I showed them a music video by the group Nickelback called "If Everyone Cared."

The video started simply enough with the band going into a studio as if for a recording session. As the music began the lyrics came in

From underneath the trees, we watch the sky

Confusing stars for satellites

I never dreamed that you'd be mine

But here we are, we're here tonight

Singing Amen, I'm alive

Singing Amen, I'm alive

As the chorus came in, the pictures suddenly shifted to words and some images of a young white man with long hair being led through a torn village of emaciated African children. Words flashed across the screen

"What would happen if everyone cared?"

If everyone cared and nobody cried

"1984. Bob Geldof, music journalist turned punk rock frontman"

If everyone loved and nobody lied

"Was inspired by a news report about"

If everyone shared and swallowed their pride

"Africa's famine epidemic"

"And began his fight against world hunger.

Then we'd see the day...

"Geldof organized the world's first global charity concert.

When nobody died

"LIVE AID"

Amen I, Amen I, Amen I, I'm Alive

> "Performances by 100 artists around the world were viewed by 1.5 billion people"

Amen I, Amen I, Amen I, I'm Alive

> "Live Aid raised 150 million British Pounds Sterling in One Day."

I heard a few "whoas" and "wows" from the students. As the video continued, lyrics were overshadowed by images and stories of everyday people who changed the world.

> "1976. Betty Williams, a receptionist and mother of two, witnessed three children killed during the political turmoil in Northern Ireland. Within two days of the tragic event, Williams obtained 6,000 signatures petitioning for peace. She then led 10,000 people on a peace march to the children's graves. The peaceful march was disrupted by protesters. One week later, Williams organized another march. This time the march was... 35,000 STRONG. Betty Williams was awarded the Nobel Peace Prize in 1976."

As these last words crossed the screen, I heard a few sniffles from the darkened audience and some students surreptitiously searching for tissues.

If everyone shared and swallowed their pride
Then we'd see the day when nobody died
If everyone cared and nobody cried...

> "1961. Two students in Portugal raised their glasses in a toast to Freedom. They were imprisoned for seven years. British lawyer Peter Benenson was shocked by the events. To rally support for the students, he wrote a letter to his local paper. The response was so overwhelming that a committee was formed to organize the campaign. It quickly turned into a worldwide movement... known today as Amnesty International."

For more information on Circle K, The Six Cents Initiative, or the Tomorrow Fund, please visit www.circlek.org..

Some of the students were now losing the fight to keep the tears from rolling down their cheeks.

And as we lie beneath the stars, we realize how small we are

If they could love like you and me, imagine what the world could be

If everyone cared...

> "1920s. A boy from a small South African village dreamt of a day when equality would prevail over his country. After years of activism, he was charged with political treason and sentenced to life in prison. His dream of equality never died. In 1990, after 27 years in prison, Nelson Rolihlahla Mandela was finally released. Mandela then led South Africa to its first ever democratic presidential election. Nearly 19 million people voted. Nelson Mandela won the election, ending the racist apartheid regime that divided South Africa for 46 years."

We'd see the day, we'd see the day, when nobody died

We'd see the day, we'd see the day, when nobody died

We'd see the day, we'd see the day, when nobody died

As the band wrapped up the recording session and started putting away their instruments, the image faded into that of a young woman marching. In the absence of music, Betty Williams' voice came through loud and clear. "We just walked right through all the stones, all the bottles, and whatever they threw. We have won a major victory."

The words then silently crossed the screen. "CHANGE THE WORLD."

Other words then appeared to fill in the remainder of my favorite quote. "Never doubt that a small group of committed people can CHANGE THE WORLD. Indeed, it is the only thing that ever has."—Margaret Mead.

For more information on Circle K, The Six Cents Initiative, or the Tomorrow Fund, please visit www.circlek.org.

When we put the lights back on, there was not a dry eye in the whole room. Some of the most stalwart people moments before had tears freely rolling down their cheeks. But these tears were not of sorrow, or sadness. They were tears of realization that they COULD do anything, that they COULD change the world. If an obscure singer could raise the equivalent of half a billion dollars in one day to relieve world hunger, if a receptionist could organize a peace march of 35,000 people, if a lawyer could cause Amnesty International to be formed almost overnight, and if a political prisoner could become president, then *what could they do?*

These were tears of the possible, these young college students understanding that they could change the world. Anything is possible. ANYTHING.

For my part, this was my singular Circle K moment, seeing the possibility of changing the world in the eyes looking back at me. I knew that through a simple video I could have a part in igniting their own fires, and over the rest of the weekend I could now help them focus and organize their passion to change the world.

Over the months that followed, there were many times I had a lot of work to do in my law practice, and there were a lot of times where it would have been easier for me to just pack it in and do only for myself and my family. But the memory of that night and the look of possibility in their eyes will make sure that I never pack things in.

This is my Circle K moment. Here follow more of these moments. And hopefully, once you've read them, you'll get out there, help change the world, and discover your own moment.

For more information on Circle K, The Six Cents Initiative, or the Tomorrow Fund, please visit www.circlek.org..

For more information on Circle K, The Six Cents Initiative, or the Tomorrow Fund,
please visit www.circlek.org.

7

*For more information on Circle K, The Six Cents Initiative, or the Tomorrow Fund,
please visit www.circlek.org..*

SECTION I:
THE STORIES

This book is organized into three parts, the first section being the longest. It is here that past and present Circle K and Kiwanis Family members submitted the moments that made them realize that serving others is and should be a way of life. It is with great hope that these stories will inspire you to help others and find your own Circle K moment.

Family

by Ashley Hedges
University of North Carolina at Chapel Hill Circle K

"You can not do all the good the world needs, but the world needs all the good you can do." --Anonymous

I first joined the Kiwanis Family as a high schooler, dismayed at my newfound community service requirement. I went to a classical high school, meaning that I had applied and chosen to attend in lieu of going to the high school I was districted to attend. Key Club began as just a resource for me, a place to gather ideas about the different kinds of community service I could do, and I stuck with the organization once I learned it was one of those "gold stars" that would appear on my transcript for college, something uniquely distinguishable to those it mattered most.

For more information on Circle K, The Six Cents Initiative, or the Tomorrow Fund, please visit www.circlek.org.

I ended my career in Key Club at the annual District Convention that concluded the year, and I can still remember to this day being in attendance at that particular event. I sat in the audience, watching candidate after candidate approach the podium to speak before the convention attendees in hopes of persuading them to gain their vote, and I have to confess, I indeed felt very out of place. The convention was more than just an election process, but indeed a great deal of emphasis is placed on selecting those who will lead the district in the coming year, as it should be. Although I understood its necessity, it served little importance to me, and I couldn't bring myself to elicit any concern for the continuation of the organization I still knew very little about.

Another portion of the convention includes attending workshops that will give you ideas for the upcoming year, and sadly I felt that same strong sense of irrelevance in many of those as well, with the exception of one: Circle K. The workshop was an introduction to the collegiate level of the Kiwanis Family, and although I was aware of it, I hadn't been fully convinced there was any reason I should continue with my time in the Kiwanis Family. As luck would have it, the leader of the workshop thought otherwise. His enthusiasm that day inspired me to at least give Circle K a chance, and I sought out the club upon my arrival at UNC Chapel Hill those first, humid days of August.

I found out at that point that the leader of my workshop, Alec Macaulay, was in fact now the International President of Circle K. This struck me with surprise, and it made a lasting impression of Circle K that I still find to hold true today; after all, when he had such a much larger commitment and other things to worry about, why was he taking the time to stop and convince little ol' me to join? Yet, Circle K has a way of bringing people together who I am convinced were just *meant* to find one another.

For more information on Circle K, The Six Cents Initiative, or the Tomorrow Fund, please visit www.circlek.org..

At the first district event I attended, I found myself in a world so different from my own. The project was the District Large Scale Service Project, and it included a weekend committed to helping the Boys and Girls Home of Lake Waccamaw, a program dedicated to renewing hope and rebuilding the lives of children and families. That weekend, our group of Circle Kers was put in charge of painting a country store at the Boys and Girls Home, since it was one of their major sources of income for their program. The building was large and the project seemed impossible to accomplish in just two short days, but the members of Circle K each picked up a brush and set to work. It was powerful to see so many students from different universities all working together for a common goal. Yes, even Carolina and Duke were working side-by-side.

Here were a group of college kids, who probably had so many other things on their plate, giving up their weekend to travel to a small community just to put in a few hours of volunteer work. Yet the thirty students that showed up that weekend accomplished so much, and through that shared experience created a bond built on laughter and hard work. You never realize how much you have in common with people so different from you until you join together with them on a task that even I have to confess I thought was impossible at first glance.

It was here too, that I met a brown-haired, blue-eyed girl, not unlike myself. I had spent the day with Amanda Lawing, sharing a ladder and painting an entire wall of the building together as we slowly came to learn more about one another. We soon realized that we were both from the same hometown of Fayetteville, NC and that we apparently looked more alike than even we realized. As we returned to the Solomon Center our first night in attendance, after a long day of painting, person after person asked us if we were in fact related. We giggled, and I insisted "No" although Amanda would first try lightheartedly to convince them that we were in fact sisters. It made sense after all, we both came from the same

For more information on Circle K, The Six Cents Initiative, or the Tomorrow Fund, please visit www.circlek.org.

13

hometown and had just chosen to attend separate colleges; she was the older, inspiring one, and I was the younger, inquisitive one.

As I continued to attend other events, I grew tiresome of opposing those who questioned, "Are you two related?" and I let Amanda answer that we were actually sisters. Yet, after a while, I found fellow Circle Kers questioning me that very same thought without Amanda standing by my side. I found myself not wanting to lie, yet I couldn't truthfully admit that we were *just* friends. At that moment, I got it; I learned what it meant to be a part of the Kiwanis Family. Amanda was, and still is, indeed my sister, and along with her, I have found a whole collection of family members I wasn't aware I had. They are all inspiring, proactive counterparts that have encouraged me in my life and been there for me when I needed them the most. And yes, my family does extend to include a bright, wonderful group of Key Clubbers who understand something that was so foreign to me when I stood in their shoes.

Yet, as my studies in both religion and philosophy at Carolina have led me to confront; I often wonder if what I do through Circle K, if the time I spend volunteering, really does matter. When asked this question, I know now that my answer, without hesitation, is "yes". In explaining this, I refer back to my first trip down to the Boys and Girls Home. I learned later that the workers arriving at the country store the Monday just after we had departed, wept tears of joy at seeing their place of work transformed. It mattered a great deal to them.

The Boys and Girls Home itself works with troubled children to restore order to their life. I wondered how much of an impact this type of organization had on the children it worked with, and I learned first hand on one of the few weekends I found myself at my own home. My mom inquired, "And where were you this weekend with Circle K? How were you trying to save the world this time?" I explained about the Boys and Girls Home, it having been my third trip down there at the time. She paused for a moment, but then grinned at the choice I had made to help those individuals. I confessed to her too about my worry that maybe what the Home was doing for those children just wasn't enough, but she evaporated my concern altogether. She answered, "You probably don't realize this, but your dad was in a similar home at one point in his life, and he credits the counselor he met there with making the positive change in turning his own life around."

I couldn't believe it; I love my dad, and I don't think he'll ever realize how proud I am of all that he has accomplished in his own life. As a previous high school drop out, he is not the kind of individual that is willing to speak about his past, because I think he still feels the pain of regret. Yet, I have seen him turn his life around entirely, and I have never known him to be anything other than a hard working individual, dedicated to consistently improving the lives of me and my brother. He attended night classes while I was younger in addition to his own job working as an IT Specialist, in order to obtain both his GED and Bachelor's Degree. He taught me at young age that my education was important, and prevented me from ever taking that commitment lightly.

If that is indeed the sort of impact that an organization like the Boys and Girls Home can have on just one individual, then I am absolutely proud to be associated with them. And if the various tasks we accomplish as we ascend there in groups of Circle Kers is what enables the Home to function, since they do run entirely on donations and community support, then I would have to say that

"Yes, what we do does matter." I think there has been a long history of individuals who understood this, who realized that we need to work at improving the world, not because we ought to, but because we *can*. I believe Anne Frank expressed this best when she stated, "How wonderful it is that nobody need wait a single moment before starting to improve the world."

For more information on Circle K, The Six Cents Initiative, or the Tomorrow Fund, please visit www.circlek.org..

Smiles Changing the World

by Heather Leah

Former President of Crossroads Kiwanis Club

"Smile!" I shouted, flashing a neon yellow poster at Seattle's bustling crowd.

I was standing in the epicenter of Pike Place Market, three thousand miles away from my home in North Carolina, trying to coax complete strangers into smiling. Nearby, a blind street musician sang about peace and harmony. Vendors shouted "Fish! Fish for sale!" from their booths. Soon, though, they noticed my sign and began to call out to passersby: *Smile!*

I grinned. This was the perfect place to raise a little change.

For more information on Circle K, The Six Cents Initiative, or the Tomorrow Fund, please visit www.circlek.org.

My three companions and I were traveling together, doing volunteer work and good deeds across the country, chasing the adolescent dream and trying to change the world. Over a month ago we'd packed our bags, left our families, and set off across the country, stopping in dozens of cities to do volunteer work and random good deeds. We were young, idealistic, and on a mission of kindness, certain that if we threw ourselves into the masses to do good work, we'd surely change the world—or at least ourselves.

Over the top of a dozen bobbing heads I saw another bright "Smile!" sign, weaving towards me through the crowd. "Hi, Amber," I said. "Getting lots of smiles?"

"Yep!" she said, arching an eyebrow, "But we need to find a way to raise some money while we're out here, too. We're seriously low on funds. At this point we won't even have enough money for gas by the end of the week. And we aren't exactly close to home."

"We could sing for change," I suggested, thinking of the street performers. "Though I'm not a very good singer."

"Yeah, that's my idea actually. Chris and Shane are down the street with their signs. We should go find them and let them know."

"Sure," I agreed, and we walked down the street, flashing "Smile!" signs at the crowds. The lure of spreading joy was far more tempting than singing for our supper.

"Some girls spreading the love, bright smiling signs," sang a guitarist as we walked past. We laughed and waved.

When we found Shane and Chris we explained the financial situation.

For more information on Circle K, The Six Cents Initiative, or the Tomorrow Fund, please visit www.circlek.org..

"Well, there are four of us, right?" said Amber. "What if we each agree to raise twenty dollars somehow before we leave Seattle tonight? That'll be eighty bucks between us."

"That doesn't sound too hard," I said, but I was already worrying. Twenty wasn't much, but I wasn't even twenty bucks worth of a performer, and I couldn't say much for Shane or Chris either.

"So we're agreed?" Yes. Yes, we consented.

The hours passed steadily, and we continued getting people to smile. It was an incredible experience. Scowling strangers passed us on the gray street, stony and intimidating. Then shared smiles transformed them into old friends. And suddenly that grouchy old lady hobbling down the street wasn't a bitter old woman, but somebody's grandmother. It was beautiful. Children smiled. A forlorn-looking homeless woman sitting on the sidewalk looked up and gave us a huge grin. "Thank you," she said. The marketplace, filled with foreign faces and separate individuals, began to fuse together into a mass of smiling people, all talking to each other about those strange kids with the yellow signs.

After a while, people began to stop and take pictures of us. Vendors offered us free fruit. We were treated like celebrities, just for getting crowds to smile!

And as the sun began the set, we found ourselves richer—but only in the spiritual sense.

We regrouped, listening to the blind musician singing about peace.

"Portland's our next stop. We have friends there. We'll be okay, we just have to keep going, I guess," said Annabelle. "Sleep in the car if we have to. Eat cheaply."

For more information on Circle K, The Six Cents Initiative, or the Tomorrow Fund, please visit www.circlek.org.

I frowned a bit. We were traveling around the country doing good deeds and volunteer work. Weren't things supposed to just sort of work out for us? How could we end this journey so soon, just because of something as mundane as money?

A sudden commotion kept me from getting lost in my own misery. A stray foot had accidentally kicked over the blind musician's money jar. We rushed to his aid, but a white-haired gentleman swooped in first. He bent over, rescuing the scattering money from the dozens of scuffling feet. We looked on, impressed. Since beginning our road trip, we'd never had someone "steal" a good deed from us. When the crisis was over, we spoke to him.

"Hi," I said. "Wow, that was really nice of you. We just wanted to, you know, thank you for doing a good deed, I guess."

"It looks like I'm not alone in my deed-doing," he said, nodding towards our signs. "What are those for?"

"Oh, we're just trying to brighten people's day."

"I'm sure you've brightened a few," he said, his expression warm and wise. "Where are you from?"

We told him of our journey, of our mission to spread kindness across the country.

His eyes lit up with a kind of nostalgia. "I understand your mission," he said with a faint smile, "I have done similar things in my youth."

"Tell us about them!" I asked hungrily.

For more information on Circle K, The Six Cents Initiative, or the Tomorrow Fund, please visit www.circlek.org..

"That," he said warmly, "Is a story for another time perhaps." He paused, examining us. His gaze seemed almost proud, as if he were a father admiring his children. "I do want to donate to this cause though. I think your mission seems noble," he said, opening his wallet.

"Oh, no, sir! Thank you, but we don't want to take your money!" Amber said, raising her hands to object.

"I insist. I want to play at least a small part in this mission," he said, pulling out a twenty dollar bill. He paused for a moment, considering. "Well, what the heck," he said and pulled out three more twenties.

Eighty dollars. We thanked him, amazed that a complete stranger would just open his wallet to four traveling kids. "Good luck on your journey," he said as we parted, "I hope to hear more about it as it continues. Please email me updates."

The sun was gone and the bitter cold of Seattle nighttime was settling in as we walked back to our car. We had a long journey ahead of us, another month at least. Somewhere along the way we'd have to raise more money or we'd be forced to start sleeping in the car. What if we ran out of gas money? What if we couldn't afford food? But God still didn't seem worried, and, remembering the face of the man who had showed us such kindness, I knew that eighty dollars was more than enough to get us home again.

A Flood of Service

by Amanda Badali

Circle K International President 07-08

When you join the Kiwanis Family, you never know when your "Kiwanis Family moment" will come. For me, it was when I was in Key Club. A senior in high school – I was serving as the District Governor to the Pennsylvania District.

Flood waters in Oakmont, Pennsylvania reached a high that has not been seen in over twenty-five years. Looking back, I am *much* happier knowing that everyone was safe at home, rather than having board members from all over try to fight the weather to attend a district meeting. I believe that everything happens for a reason; while it was unfortunate that the District Board Meeting had to be cancelled, perhaps it was for the best.

For more information on Circle K, The Six Cents Initiative, or the Tomorrow Fund, please visit www.circlek.org.

On that Friday, my grandparents and I drove out to the airport to pick up our International Trustee, Austin. Instead of the usual forty-five minute drive, it took us three and a half hours. After I met up with him, we loaded his baggage into the trunk and started to head back to Oakmont. We were almost home, making it the whole way to Verona, the neighboring town.

There is a viaduct that connects Oakmont and Verona and it was closed due to flood damage. We attempted to take Plum Street, a back road, and it was closed as well. We were less than a mile from my house, yet could not get into my town.

My grandparents drove around, looking for another way to get in. The rain was coming down so hard that we could barely see out the windows – it was unlike anything I had ever seen before. We tried to go around Oakmont and come down another road, but it was blocked off too. I thought we would never get home, it was *that* bad. At this point, we were all really frustrated and worried.

After another hour or so driving around, we finally found a way into Oakmont. I can honestly say that I have NEVER been more relieved to be in my hometown. What should have been forty-five minutes out and another forty-five minutes back, turned into a trip totaling over six and half hours. I came home to find that my basement had flooded and my parents had to move furniture to clean the water. However, the damage done to my house was minimal compared to others in my town.

The next day, the local board members from the west-side of Pennsylvania were planning to meet and discuss some committee work. We had intended to eat dinner and go over everything that we could. That meeting became a last priority.

For more information on Circle K, The Six Cents Initiative, or the Tomorrow Fund, please visit www.circlek.org..

Riverview High School Key Club received a call from the Oakmont Borough, asking our assistance with helping the flood damage. After a meeting with some town council members, we headed to the high school to call all of our Key Club Members. Then the local board members, Austin, and myself went up to the Oakmont Commons, the small housing community on the top of the hill. We met up with dozens of members of the Riverview Key Club, as well as some past Key Clubbers that came to help. Ricky, a past Key Clubber, drove us around to get extra supplies. Throughout the day, he used his strength to help move the water-soaked carpet.

Key Clubbers did everything from ripping up carpet to moving furniture, passing out emergency information, mopping, distributing food, and more. Thousands upon thousands of dollars of damage was made by the muddy waters.

I was helping to wash out mud in what once was a living room of some woman's house. We had to hose out every room and closet on the first floor and then mop out the water as best as we could. I started to remove picture frames off a shelf so that they could be taken upstairs away from all of the mess. As I held the picture in my hand, I looked down to see a girl that was from my school. She was on the color guard squad with me, and we had recently got her to join Key Club. I thought "OH MY GOODNESS! Is this her house?"—and before I realized I said that out loud, the woman who we were helping responded, "Yes, I'm her mother."

As a four-year Key Clubber and proud member of the Kiwanis Family, I have never been more touched in my life. Often times, we find ourselves serving people we have never met and will never see again. Here, I found myself inside my peer's house. Talk about breathtaking.

For more information on Circle K, The Six Cents Initiative, or the Tomorrow Fund, please visit www.circlek.org.

We went from house to house, helping as much as we could. A woman in a van stopped a group of us and asked if we were the volunteers. When we responded that we were, she smiled with tears in her eyes. This was followed by two beautiful words—"Thank You."

She fought to hold back the tears. And you know what? I have never been more proud of the Kiwanis Family.

We came across an older man with no friends or extended family, just his daughter. He was divorced. Everything in his house was ruined—there was barely anything that we could salvage. He kept asking us what he should do or what he could save. We had to keep him calm as we tried to clean out his house. Both father and daughter were repeatedly urged to go get something to eat and find some clothes so that they could safely stay in a local hotel. It was nearly impossible to convince the man to leave behind his home.

A couple of us left to get some more mops, trash bags and sponges. We also stopped at a local church to pick up food to distribute. I walked up and down the streets with a few of my fellow Key Club members, offering chicken nuggets, sandwiches, muffins, pastries, pop and water to everyone and anyone. I cannot even begin to explain how grateful people were when they we handed them all this food.

"Does it cost anything?"

"No, ma'am."

"Really?"

"Yes, it's free."

"What? Oh, thank you! Thank you so much!"

For more information on Circle K, The Six Cents Initiative, or the Tomorrow Fund, please visit www.circlek.org..

People graciously accepted the food. One man asked if we were going to "receive wings" for our deeds. Needless to say, we are not angels – we are simply teenagers that stepped in when our community needed us the most.

For more information on Circle K, The Six Cents Initiative, or the Tomorrow Fund, please visit www.circlek.org.

For more information on Circle K, The Six Cents Initiative, or the Tomorrow Fund, please visit www.circlek.org..

It's Not About Beary:
The Story of a Teddy Bear

by Ali Kira Grotkowski
University of Alberta Circle K

During my first year as a CKI member, I was having a very difficult fall semester at university. Not only did I fail all my midterms, but they were all held the same week. If it wasn't for CKI members and projects to convince me that there was more to life than academic success, I probably wouldn't have passed all of those classes, let alone finished my Bachelors of Science and gone on to complete a Bachelors of Arts degree. In fact if it wasn't for CKI, I'm sure that I wouldn't have the self-confidence I have now, nor my determination to continue my education and follow my dreams.

For more information on Circle K, The Six Cents Initiative, or the Tomorrow Fund, please visit www.circlek.org.

One project that helped turn my semester around was the Uncles and Aunts at Large Christmas party. Held early each December, it was a gathering of children, their families and their respective Uncles or Aunts: adult role models who step in through this organization to provide positive influences in their lives. Featuring kid-friendly food (hot dogs, orange pop, beans, tater-tots etc.) and live entertainment, the event was a joy. A generous woman with a world-welcoming smile greeted families as they entered, providing hand-knitted mittens and draw prize tickets, and others guided families to the tables, pointing out CKI's corner for the kids' enjoyment.

This corner was where all the colouring books were stored. It was also where we provided two things: face painting and balloon animals. Skilled balloon artists since the beginning of the year, we were kept occupied with those two pursuits all afternoon. If we weren't great at face painting at the beginning of the afternoon, we were certainly skilled by the end. The kids were great at pointing out flaws and insisted that we fix any mistakes that we made. I remember painting a gold star on the cheek of a two-month old baby, and complicated reindeer antlers on many children's foreheads. Perhaps the most popular decoration was a set of Christmas bells to adorn a proud parent's face, convinced to participate in the face painting by a glowing child.

One particularly memorable moment was when an eight-year-old boy approached me, face red, tears dripping from his eyes. He thanked me for his happiest moment this year, since he wouldn't be getting anything for Christmas. He wanted to give me a hug and showed me the drawing he had made, after I had painted the Edmonton Oilers logo on his cheek.

For more information on Circle K, The Six Cents Initiative, or the Tomorrow Fund, please visit www.circlek.org..

This fun continued until the jolly ol' elf arrived, presents in tow. The crowd serenaded Santa with popular Christmas carols before he sat down on his throne on stage and began to distribute gifts, the only ones some children would receive that year. Each age group approached the stage, from youngest to oldest, each leaving with happy expressions, even the loudest teens. Then, they called us up, the volunteers, to sit upon Santa's lap and receive presents.

I approached the stage. Almost embarrassed, I walked up the steps toward Santa, wondering why we too HAD to go on stage. "What do you want for Christmas?" Santa asked. I don't remember what I answered that year, but every year since I've received what I desired. This Santa knew what I needed most, however, and presented me with one of the largest wrapped gifts when I left the stage.

One of the kids implored, "Open it!" So I did, finding an enormous red stuffed Teddy Bear, whom I've since named Beary. My favorite colour, he was soft and the perfect size to hug. After cleaning up, sending all the extra gifts back to charitable organizations, and saying good bye for another year, I carried my bear home by public transit and settled in for final exams and the rest of my semester, refreshed and reminded of the great difference I could make in someone's life. It isn't every day that the very kids you're entertaining, thank you with tears in their young eyes.

It wasn't until long afterward, that I realized just how special it was to have a teddy bear in my life. Any time I was feeling alone or unloved, there Beary was to hug and console me. The number of tears I've shed in silence holding Beary in my arms would fill a pond. But each time I'm also able to remember the difference I can make in the lives of others, and how important it is to volunteer my time. I'll always remember the children I've helped at these Uncles and Aunts at Large Christmas parties, partially because

For more information on Circle K, The Six Cents Initiative, or the Tomorrow Fund, please visit www.circlek.org.

Beary sits on my couch to comfort me when I'm not having a particularly great day. If it weren't for reminders such as these, I wouldn't be the person I am today. After all, Beary reminds me that I can make a difference.

So, while it is a story of a teddy bear, it's not about Beary. It's also so much more significant than people served or money raised. Because of small projects like this one, I've done many more projects on larger scale. I've helped many and done more, but it's the reminder of small projects like this one that keeps me going. This project made a difference for me. It made a difference for the children we helped. And both those reasons are why I continue on today, doing what I can to help. After all, helping others also helped me.

For more information on Circle K, The Six Cents Initiative, or the Tomorrow Fund, please visit www.circlek.org..

Finding H.O.P.E. with Jonathan

by Minerva Thai
Duke University Circle K

He looked up at me and smiled a childish grin of innocence. With his arms around my legs, as high as they could reach, he snuggled his head against the baggy folds of my sweatshirt's pocket and called me Mommy. Then, in the blink of an eye, he was gone and all I heard were his quick receding footsteps, his breathless giggle, and "you can't catch me!" The chase was on.

Little Jonathan— kindergartner and heart stealer. He was an endearing five year old whose brother was a part of the after-school homework program I had helped establish at H.O.P.E., a non-profit organization geared towards breaking the generational cycle of poverty, abuse, and other disadvantages, and with Key Club. It was 2006 and I had been volunteering there for two years, eventually achieving junior board membership. Though I had been

For more information on Circle K, The Six Cents Initiative, or the Tomorrow Fund, please visit www.circlek.org.

around John and his older brother a few times before, it wasn't until that day that I finally spent quality time with him. In previous encounters, I had been busy running around and organizing the homework program but with its development and growth of volunteers, I had to withdraw myself into administrative and secretarial duties. I worked on the computer every Tuesday while other volunteers from my Key Club did the actual tutoring. John was too young to have any substantial homework which required tutoring. This left the two of us, one day, without any person to interact with but one another.

I remember finishing all of my work early and finding the tutoring room at full capacity. When I came back into the office, there was John playing by himself amongst the stuffed animals. I made my way towards the child and asked if he wanted to play. Immediately, he popped up and hugged me, smiling sweetly. I had no idea that a game of tag would ensue. We weaved between the adults in other rooms, acting as little children do when they are lost deep within their own worlds. I was no longer a high school student but another kindergartner on a mission to find my giggling friend. However, the moments right after I caught John, I transformed once again but at those times, into a ruthless tickling monster who would torture the child until he begged and pleaded.

When we had finished our tiring games of tag, we proceeded to take advantage of the kids' corner furnished with donated knickknacks and toys. There was a puzzle which John felt had to be completed so we sorted out the pieces and got down on our knees, searching for the pieces that fit. I asked him every so often what animals we were discovering as we finished parts of the puzzle – pigs, roosters, cows, and sheep appeared. Unfortunately, when we had run out of pieces, there were some holes in the picture. It seemed that the donated puzzle had been given without all of the pieces. I was disappointed but what stood out even more to me was how accepting John was of the situation.

For more information on Circle K, The Six Cents Initiative, or the Tomorrow Fund, please visit www.circlek.org..

"Uh oh, we're missing pieces John. I'm sorry we couldn't finish it all"

He only looked at me with his bright eyes and said, "It's okay. I can still see the aminals."

I thought about what he said and his family's situation. He had an older brother and a mother who I would occasionally see pushing a shopping cart on the streets with things. She worked hard all day but never neglected her children. She would receive supplies from H.O.P.E. but did not take them as hand-outs; she always came back in her free time to volunteer as well. Before I could think too much about John's life however, he grabbed a book and ran over to my lap. He sat down and told me to read him a story. He barely knew how to read so I worked with him on the words, and we enjoyed a story about a lost rabbit. Eventually John lost interest but I encouraged him to continue reading with me. When we had finished the tale, he snuggled into my sweater and told me he was hungry.

Then immediately John jumped up and started patting his stomach which he puffed out by throwing his shoulders back.

"I want to be FAT!"

"Why would you want to be fat?" I was not prepared for the answer.

"Because kids who have food are fat, and I'm always hungry."

I could not abstain from thinking once again about his situation but this time, the realization hit hard. I had learned through academic study that certain impoverished areas in the world valued weight and held obesity as a sign of prosperity rather than unhealthiness. Being fat meant one ate well. It did not occur to me, however, that this applied to people everywhere who were in sordid situations. Reading about it in a textbook was nothing compared to seeing it in person. I had helped through many volunteers events people who needed food, warmth, and a place to stay. Yet, I had never seen or spoken to any one of those people. Here before me though was a little boy who was energetic and loveable but suffered from what I had read about. He already knew what teachers had to teach us – being fat meant one ate well. He knew this because he did not eat as often as I did; he knew this because he was aware of how little food his mother could provide.

"Well do you mean you want to be fat or that you're just hungry?"

"Both!"

"Let's get you a snack or something."

I led John to the volunteer snacks area and showed him which were healthier than the others but he was adamant about his favorite – Oreos. Then I told him that being fat did not mean being healthy and convinced him to share fruit snacks with me. We went back to the office and snacked while walking. At first he just happened to follow me but then turned it into a game. I maneuvered around, pretending to want to lose him. Then he grabbed onto my legs and giggled, "I'm going to kiss you!"

For more information on Circle K, The Six Cents Initiative, or the Tomorrow Fund, please visit www.circlek.org..

Feigning disgust, I tried to shake him off and asked him why. His reply – "I want to kiss my mommy." I ran off when he let go so we fell into another game of tag but this time, whenever John reached me, he would try to climb up and plant a wet kiss on my cheek. Eventually, I could not last against his youthful energy and let him have his wish. Yet, I had to know why he insisted on calling me his mommy. The answer was simple though: I took care of him.

When we were done with all of our fun and games, it seemed that the tutoring in the other room finished as well. His brother Andrew emerged and so did his mother. She thanked me for teaching and spending time with him; I could only remain cross-legged on the floor where John and I had been, thinking about how he taught me more than I probably taught him.

It wasn't his fault that his mother had to work laboriously every day but he suffered from it. The influence of others not even present in his life still remained – the father who left him was still there as an oppressor. I immensely respected his mother who made sure her children finished their homework and did not starve, even if they were often hungry. When they were sick, she would take time off; when they were home, she would spend time with them. I learned from John his acceptance of his situation and how it did not deter him from being an amazing person. He did not pity himself but rather, had fun with what he had. Every day that I went to H.O.P.E., I would enter excited to see John again because whenever he was there, he would leap up from wherever he was and throw himself onto me with a flying hug. I learned to appreciate more of what I had and what I could offer because I could be a friend to the boy whose family was often busy trying to make sure everyone was okay. I could be his playmate when his brother was learning math. I learned from John his dreams and desires. Most importantly of all, I learned that one person can make a difference in the world.

For more information on Circle K, The Six Cents Initiative, or the Tomorrow Fund, please visit www.circlek.org.

For more information on Circle K, The Six Cents Initiative, or the Tomorrow Fund, please visit www.circlek.org..

Building the Future

by Megan Niehaus
Ball State University CKI

Many Circle K members have a moment or memory in the line of service that has stuck with them for years after the project ended. It is these moments that keep the spirit of community service alive and strong in the hearts of our members. Although my moment came years after I found myself immersed in (and some might say addicted to) the Kiwanis Family, the little girl I met in St. Louis, Missouri has forever had her impression stamped on my heart.

For more information on Circle K, The Six Cents Initiative, or the Tomorrow Fund, please visit www.circlek.org.

One of the most amazing Kiwanis Family experiences came to me in the form of serving on the Large Scale Service Project Committee in 2004. Through this opportunity, I met Circle K members from all across the organization who were dedicated to bettering the world one child, one community at a time. After months of online meetings, late-night phone calls and instant message conversations, creating, distributing, and coordinating promotional materials and events, and laying the groundwork for what we believed would be one of the most exciting Large Scale Service Projects yet, we arrived in St. Louis to build four libraries around the city.

Over a hundred Kiwanis family members from around the world poured into the hotel with levels of enthusiasm unseen to this day. We all understood the work ahead of us, but we also all knew what it meant to come together for one colossal project that makes an impact on the lives of more than just a few individuals. Our task was to build libraries – four in fact. As a member of the planning committee, I was responsible for overseeing the construction of a library in a YWCA classroom in a low-income neighborhood of St. Louis.

We brought with us books donated by Kiwanis family members from around the world. After many Home Depot runs for wood, paint, brushes, and miscellaneous tools, all of the supplies were in place. Individuals chose projects to work on – categorizing and organizing books, painting the room, assembling shelving units, and painting the shelves – and immediately dove right into their tasks. I had never seen so many people come together so swiftly and willingly to accomplish a common goal. To see the before and after pictures of the classroom still astounds me. We, the 25 of us assigned to that site, completely transformed a bland, empty classroom into a vibrant area that was not only welcoming but also encouraged students to read. They now had easy access to books on various reading levels across many topics and a comfortable, safe place to read.

After three days of arduous labor, it was time to reveal the library to the kids. Circle K members, children, parents, and YWCA volunteers and workers crowded the hallway as the ribbon was cut to officially open the library for business. Like a river rushes through a broken dam, children poured into the library with ecstatic grins and palpable energy. You've heard the phrase "like a little kid in a candy shop?" Imagine that. Most ran from shelf to shelf to check out what new books they had. Some ran off towards Ricky Reader, our own Alabama-grown reading mascot, but one child in particular stayed back from the rest.

This little girl with bright brown eyes seemed overcome with some sort of emotion, but I couldn't tell what. Was she afraid of getting trampled in this group of people? Was she really shy? Was she in some way hurt that she could not walk into the room? I walked over to this little girl, whose name I never got, crouched down to her height, and asked if she was ok. She just nodded. "Hmmm," I thought as I stood back up. I remained near the girl in hopes that she would soon share what had gotten her so worked up, and within moments, it was as if she read my mind. I'll never forget how I was looking out across all the other students in the room when this little girl, this little bit of magic in today's world, tugged at my shirt, looked up into my face, and said, "Thanks for the *wibrary*." After a moment in silence, she wandered off to check out the selection and get settled for a read-aloud.

For more information on Circle K, The Six Cents Initiative, or the Tomorrow Fund, please visit www.circlek.org.

It was in this defining moment as I watched her walk away that I realized what the Kiwanis family and helping others is all about. We are given a gift in life – time to spend how we choose and the ability to make decisions that affect other people. I chose to give up not only a week of my time for the project in St. Louis but also countless hours of planning, and I would have done so freely without this defining moment. But this thirty-second conversation with a six year-old girl truly changed my life. I realized that time and resources are precious. I realized that the littlest things can make a big difference. The fact that this girl was so in awe of the library we built shows that many kids are happy just to know you've taken the time to spend time with them. Helping others is not about the good feeling volunteers get at the end of the day, the free food that often accompanied projects, or the recognition they may get. It's about knowing that you've made a positive, lasting impact on another individual.

For more information on Circle K, The Six Cents Initiative, or the Tomorrow Fund, please visit www.circlek.org..

Raising the Roof

by Jeffrey G. Marsocci
Raleigh Kiwanis Club

I sat in my office after the call, wondering if it would work.

In addition to the 20,000 other things I volunteered for with Kiwanis, I was also on the Carolinas District of Kiwanis committee for the Boys and Girls Home at Lake Waccamaw, NC. The Home literally puts a roof over the heads of children who have no place to go, and the now the roof of the Kiwanis Cottage was falling apart. And the Home couldn't afford a new roof.

I had spoken with Larry Hewett at the Boys and Girls Home, and had asked me how they could get $15,000 for a new roof. I answered him with another question: "How much is needed for the materials to put on a new roof?"

For more information on Circle K, The Six Cents Initiative, or the Tomorrow Fund, please visit www.circlek.org.

"$15,000," Larry responded as more of a question than a statement, not really understanding what I was getting at.

"No, how much are the *materials*, not the final cost," I said. "I assume that the $15,000 is for everything, including the roofers and other labor."

"Well, yes," Larry said.

"What I really need is a breakdown of each item needed, right down to how much each box of roofing nails cost, and how many are needed; how much a package of shingles cost, and how many are needed; costs for all of the materials, including tax," I said. "If you can get me a breakdown of all of those items, all-inclusive, then I think I would have a much easier time getting Kiwanis clubs to give money for items needed rather than some amorphous $15,000 goal."

"Well, Jeff, that's all well and good, but how are we going to get the roof put on?" Larry asked.

"We have about 12,000 Kiwanians in the Carolinas District, and a decent number of them have worked on Habitat houses in the past," I said. "I think we'll have enough Kiwanis talent to handle the project without having to raise money to hire a roofing crew. Just give me a four day weekend to get the job done and I'll get the people."

That was three days ago, and Larry got me the list and dates this morning. We need a little more than $7,900 in materials, and then we needed find Kiwanians skilled in working on roofs. I put all of the information I could into an e-mail to every Kiwanis club president and secretary asking for donations and asking for volunteers. I breathed a sigh realizing that I was committing myself yet again to another project, and this was taking on a risk. How would Kiwanis respond, really?

For more information on Circle K, The Six Cents Initiative, or the Tomorrow Fund, please visit www.circlek.org..

I hit the "send" button, and then went home for the day.

***

The next morning, I got into the office, warmed up the computer, and started to get the day organized. In checking the e-mail, I already had a few responses waiting. A few hundred dollars from one club, another telling me they would bring it to the club at their meeting today…

There was a knock at the door, which was a little strange. Being in an office complex, people usually just come in, but it *was* 7:30 in the morning. I opened the door and a gentleman I had never seen before asked if I was Jeffrey.

"Yes, can I help you with something?"

"Oh, good," he said. "I didn't know if you would be here this early in the morning, but I thought I'd take a chance. I got your e-mail just before going to my Kiwanis meeting last night, and they approved a $1,000 donation. I wanted to drop off the check since I was going to be in Raleigh anyway."

I smiled and thanked him profusely. Less than 24 hours, and we already had $1,000 in hand.

***

For more information on Circle K, The Six Cents Initiative, or the Tomorrow Fund, please visit www.circlek.org.

Oh, boy.

It was twilight on the Wednesday before the project. We had gotten all of the money we needed, and staff members at the Boys and Girls Home had purchased everything. We had about 20 or so volunteers committed to come at various times throughout the four days of the project. The Lillington Kiwanis Club came in a little late on donating money for the materials since we already had enough, and while they really wanted to help with the labor, too many of their members were not able to come. Instead, they responded with the best gift anyone could think of. They dug really deep into their funds and came up with $5,000 to hire a professional roofing crew to help us, and they sent Kiwanis member and contractor Connie Mack Johnson to supervise them.

Yes, when the need was greatest, Kiwanis responded. We received all of the money we needed, and then some. We had the materials. People were bringing their tools. We had the labor. The Boys and Girls Home had given us use of an empty housing facility for the volunteers, and they were providing meals for us. Everything we needed was right there.

And now that I was actually standing in front of the Kiwanis Cottage, I just hoped that we would be able to get the job done in four days.

"OK, you'll have plenty of time to see the roof this weekend," my wife Kathy said. "We need to get something to eat and make things ready for the rest of the volunteers when they get here tomorrow."

While Kathy was my wife, she was also president of the Kiwanis Young Professionals of Raleigh, and tonight she was thinking about taking care of the team. "Let's go," I said.

For more information on Circle K, The Six Cents Initiative, or the Tomorrow Fund, please visit www.circlek.org..

***

I never used to have a problem with heights. I don't know if I saw one too many movies with a shaking camera focused on an actor or actress walking on the edge of a slippery building, then panning over the side to see that they were 40 stories up. My heart was thumping in my chest and I kept leaning back from the edge of the roof as if by even coming close to standing up straight, I'd fall off the side.

It didn't really matter that I was only about 10 feet off the ground and could probably jump it if I wanted to. It didn't matter that as a young boy I used to love going up on the roof with my grandfather whenever he had to fix something. It didn't even matter that during college I had jumped off a metal trellis 60 feet high into 20 feet of water. I was trying to hold down the panic. The work *had* to get done.

I walked back up to the apex of the roof and started scraping shingles off to the side and it was approaching Noon. One of the professional roofers walked over, smiled, picked up a big pile of the shingles I had scraped off, and walked calmly to the other side of the building to throw it into the dumpster. As I pulled my hat off and wiped the sweat off my face, I looked around and saw all of the volunteers either scraping away shingles or ripping off pieces of rotted wood that needed replacing.

For more information on Circle K, The Six Cents Initiative, or the Tomorrow Fund, please visit www.circlek.org.

A few minutes later, I had scraped up another pile and brought my own pile to the dumpster this time. Walking a lot slower and more carefully than my roofer friend. Things were really moving along in getting the old roof off, but the real test would be getting the new shingles on over the next three and a half days. As I walked back, the professional roofers were starting to lay the tar paper down and were getting some of the packets of shingles. Maybe we could get... CRACK!

I started to fall to the side and reached out to steady myself, almost completely losing my balance. I had visions of rolling off the side of the roof and falling to the ground. But I quickly gained my balance back and looked down. My foot had broken partway through a rotted board, but it stopped short of going all the way through. Yeah, this was going to be a rough day.

***

It was getting towards the end of the work day for Thursday, mostly because the professional roofing crew had to head back to Fayetteville. Then I got the good news/bad news/bad news. The good news was that Connie Mack thought we would be done by the end of the day Friday, a full two days ahead of time. Looking at the work we had accomplished, it was possible. We had the entire old roof scraped off and about a third of the shingles down. Plus it was kind of hard to argue with a guy who had done so much construction in his time that his rough hands were absolutely huge. We actually took a very interesting picture of Connie holding his hand up and open with Kathy doing the same thing right in front of his hand. Kathy's spread out fingers fit in his palm.

The first of the bad news was—regardless of whether or not we were done, the roofing crew was done at 5 p.m. tomorrow. That would cut out about half of our workforce, but again, we'd still be able to get the roof done by the end of the weekend, weather permitting. The second and worse of the bad news was it was starting to look like rain. And we had no tarps. If it rained, we would simply have to wait it out and hope that there would not be too so much damage that we'd have to start the roofing over and do some clean up inside the cottage. That was definitely not something we needed.

I stared at the roof a little longer before dragging my tired and aching body to the dining hall for dinner. Despite almost falling through the roof and feeling like I would fall over the side a few times, and despite the threat of rain, I felt more physically alive than I had in years.

***

I woke up the next morning to my alarm and tried to jump out of bed. I made it out of bed but my muscles screaming at me made me realized I should have probably gone a little more slowly. Nonetheless, I quickly threw on yesterday's sweaty clothes and started putting on my shoes. "Where are you going," Kathy asked from the other twin bed in the tiny dorm-style room we were assigned.

"I'll be right back," I said through the closing door. I walked quickly through the dining area and outside. I lifted my hands into the air in victory and did a little dance of thanks. "Yes! Yes! Yes!" It had not rain during the night.

For more information on Circle K, The Six Cents Initiative, or the Tomorrow Fund, please visit www.circlek.org.

***

After a quick shower and change into clean clothes, the other volunteers slowly got up and started moving. From the look of things, I wasn't the only one needing Advil this morning. Kathy and I wolfed breakfast down, put on the tool belts, and went to the Kiwanis Cottage. Connie Mack was already there getting the professional roofing crew organized, and his smile echoed mine that we escaped rain from the night before.

I decided to keep my feet mostly on the ground for the day, running tools and supplies up and down the ladder. Thankfully, we had a machine lift for the heaviest items, and I had to wonder how people carried 75 pound packages of shingles up and down ladders before these lifts existed. Still, I managed to haul these packages and heavier items around to the places they were needed, and in between I lead the ground cleanup efforts.

Between bringing supplies up the ladder, and picking up nails and broken shingles from the ground, I got into such a tightly focused zone that I lost track of what was going on. As I reached down to pick up a piece of paper, I felt a tap on my shoulder. I looked up and Connie Mack Johnson was grinning. "Take a look," he said.

What I saw was amazing. About ninety-percent of the roof was done. "It's about lunch time," Connie Mack said. "We could push through, but I'd rather give people a break and something to eat, and then we can knock this one out of the park when we get back."

For more information on Circle K, The Six Cents Initiative, or the Tomorrow Fund, please visit www.circlek.org..

I stood there stunned. It now seemed ridiculous to even think that we might not be able to get the roof done in four days, and at midway through the second day we were only about an hour away from being done. "Yeah, if you think that's best, let's do it," I told Connie Mack.

***

After a few pictures and a trip to the restaurant for some of the best Eastern North Carolina Barbecue around, we put in another hour of work to finish that roof around 2 in the afternoon. I stood there and could not be more proud of Kiwanis. When the call went out for help, Kiwanis responded. Not just with money but with our own muscle and sweat. And on top of that, we finished in less than half the time.

As I looked out over the tired crew members, they were also beaming with pride. Just then, Larry Hewett came over to give his thanks. "But," he said, "since we have you here, do you think you could help us with another project? The Fellowship Hall needs painting. We have all of the supplies, and it should only take another hour or two at the most."

I just smiled and looked at my fellow Kiwanians. "Well, we were going to be here for two more days," Kathy said. "Another few hours can't hurt."

And so Kiwanis got to work.

For more information on Circle K, The Six Cents Initiative, or the Tomorrow Fund, please visit www.circlek.org.

***

That was back in 2003, and I have had plenty of opportunities to go back to the Boys and Girls Home at Lake Waccamaw with Circle K over the years. Each Spring and each Fall, the Carolinas District of Circle K brings members from all across North and South Carolina to help the Home with various projects for its District Large Scale Service Project. The Home has also been good enough to loan our district space each year for Circle K to hold its District Officer Training Conference. I've developed many new service and fellowship memories over those years. But each time I'm there I stop by the Kiwanis Cottage, look at the roof, and smile.

For more information on Circle K, The Six Cents Initiative, or the Tomorrow Fund, please visit www.circlek.org..

The Meaning of *Thank You*

by Patricia Guzman
UCLA Circle K

I never imagined the streets of West Hollywood could have such a profound effect on me. Whenever I heard about the West Hollywood Food Coalition project, I had pictured a spacious kitchen, an abundance of donated food, and a few homeless people sporadically stationed on the streets. I imagined us coming in and handing out perfectly packaged paper bagged dinners and having enough to give seconds. When I stepped out of the car that evening with the sun coming down, reality shook me, woke me into existence for the first time, leaving me trembling like a leaf.

For more information on Circle K, The Six Cents Initiative, or the Tomorrow Fund, please visit www.circlek.org.

"Where am I?" I thought, looking around at dilapidating factories, buildings that smelled of abandon, a large moving truck parking up ahead. That was the West Hollywood Food Coalition crew: a blonde woman comfortably dressed in a tie-dyed shirt and Capri's, a short man with a tan face, and tall man who I later learned was named Moe. As soon as we told them we were from Circle K, Moe began to delegate work and we began unloading the truck. The people we were serving had already begun to wait nearby on sidewalks they called home. A man in a wheel chair played with his dog, while three other men leaned against the fence smoking cigarette butts.

"It's going to be busy," Moe said. "You two can serve juice and soup," he told my friend Lili and I. Lili had been there before, so she took soup duties. I had begun to pour gallons of orange juice into paper cups when the sun was leaving its last traces on the polluted sidewalk. "Okay, we're ready to start," said the little man. A line began to form, not just the kind outside of public restrooms, the kind you wait to see Mickey Mouse when you're five. But this wasn't fantasy, and it was far from familiar feelings of childhood, it was about survival.

My hands shook, and I hoped nobody would notice. I wasn't afraid of these people, I was afraid for them. I saw in each of them someone I may have known throughout my life. Some were aging, and wore the years of living on the streets in their sun burned wrinkles. Others were my parents' age, and I wondered if they had children. I saw a young man who looked about my age; he could have been in my Philosophy class for all I knew. Instead, he was strangely out of place here, so young and full of life. I looked down the line that seemed endless, my mind not fully comprehending what I saw. "That's enough juice for now," the little man said. I realized I had poured too many cups and the table was full.

For more information on Circle K, The Six Cents Initiative, or the Tomorrow Fund, please visit www.circlek.org..

I switched jobs with Lili, and began to pour soup into Styrofoam cups. The disparity between my lifestyle and theirs grew when I realized my extreme attention to neatness. But as I looked around me, I was the only one in the crew who even noticed the soup dripping down the Styrofoam, or the chicken piled on the same plate as desserts. In my world of overly organized planning and meals, using the same plate and no utensils was unthinkable. But this was now my world too and I began to see the struggles these people faced everyday. I poured as much soup as I could fit into the tiny cup.

I smiled, perhaps too much, trying to hide overwhelming sadness with anything I could offer. A Hispanic man talking to another had just come from work; he looked too clean to belong here. Yet he was here for dinner too. Looking at that man I was struck with the familiar scene of alcoholic men I had seen on the streets as a child, my father roaming among them. I felt a lump in my throat, but smiled as the man thanked me in Spanish. "*Gracias*," he said. Thank you. I thought about my father, a man in his fifties, divorced after years of working jobs he couldn't keep and escapades out on the streets like this man here. I could read this man's story like a book: wife and kids, some small paying construction job nearby, an act he played like dress-up in-between his real full-time marriage to a bottle of vodka. But at that moment, his gratitude told a different story—a more hopeful story.

Looking down at the large pot of soup, I realized it was almost empty. I scraped the last of it into a cup, feeling as much guilt as if I had eaten it all myself. I kept wondering if I had given someone too much, and kicking myself for not rationing better. I couldn't even look them in the eyes when they asked for more. The little man gave them chicken instead, but I felt awful. On the drive home, I thought about what I could have brought with me: all my extra change, food from the dining hall, water from my mini-fridge. I

For more information on Circle K, The Six Cents Initiative, or the Tomorrow Fund, please visit www.circlek.org.

wanted to give these people the world, but who was I to think I held that in my hands.

When I came back to my room that night, I was in shock. I sat there at my desk, hungry myself after a long day, but too guilty to eat. Eventually I went to the dining hall, but I had no appetite. I saw a guy a few tables away, and I thought about the young man I had seen out on the streets. Back in my room, I told my roommate and a few friends about what I had experienced, but I couldn't put it to words. I couldn't translate the smell of smoke in the air mixed with dirt, or the empty stares of the people, not even the words mouthed clearly: *thank you.*

For more information on Circle K, The Six Cents Initiative, or the Tomorrow Fund, please visit www.circlek.org..

Want to Save a Life?

by Melissa Summer
Furman University Circle K

"Have some spare change? Want to save a life?"

As I recruited support for the Six Cents Initiative at the Circle K table in Furman University's student center, I felt like a broken record. I must admit that I dislike relying upon emotional blackmail, but my parroted attention-grabber was a truthful appeal. For a nickel and a penny, we could provide oral rehydration packets for children in countries that lack water purification systems. For six cents, we could save a life.

For more information on Circle K, The Six Cents Initiative, or the Tomorrow Fund, please visit www.circlek.org.

Apparently, Furman University responds well to legitimate emotional blackmail.

Our Circle K members united to prepare our collection devices (water bottles turned into piggy banks), propaganda (water droplet signs for campus distribution), and war strategy (we challenged the various housing locations on campus to raise the most money). We stationed ourselves at a table in the University Center every day for a week, and we also canvassed residences to adopt unwanted coins collecting dust in forgotten jars.

I knew the Six Cents Initiative was a worthy cause: I had no idea what to expect from the Furman community. On the first day, we were unsure if we should remove our sign from our table to prevent vandalism. I opted to leave it on the table the second day, merely because my hands were too full to carry it.

Given my fears about the sign, the sight that met me the following morning shocked me. An anonymous donor left a pile of change on our table. I had worried about leaving a cheap—but lovingly decorated—piece of poster board on our table for fear of its disappearance, yet someone trusted our community enough to leave money on the table. And there it was: no one wanted to steal it. They wanted to help.

This one simple act, which recurred several other mornings that week, touched me powerfully. In a world with such focus on the negative, we easily see the worst in human nature. Deep down, however, we all know good exists—we just have to be brave enough to take a risk and trust. Six cents did more than save a life. It reinstated my faith in others who also desire to help those in need. Seeing those coins heaped on the table reminded me that we were not in this mission alone. Furman wanted to help. When some donors felt guilty that they could give only the few pennies in their possession, I stressed that every little bit can make a difference.

For more information on Circle K, The Six Cents Initiative, or the Tomorrow Fund, please visit www.circlek.org..

By the end of the week, we had raised $500. We saved over 8,330 lives.

Little things make a difference. A donation of only six cents can save a life, but a kind action as simple as smiling at a stranger or holding open a door for someone whose hands are full is just as meaningful. You never know if the stranger with whom you shared a smile was having a rough day and feeling alone, and perhaps your simple act of kindness provided a glimpse of relief. You never know if after holding open that door, the person with full hands was on her way to donate books to a local children's literacy program. Little acts of kindness are the foundations of larger efforts to leave a long-lasting imprint on the community. One of my favorite quotes expresses this idea: "You cannot do all the good the world needs, but the world needs all the good you can do."

Have some spare time? Want to change a life? Welcome to Circle K.

For more information on Circle K, The Six Cents Initiative, or the Tomorrow Fund, please visit www.circlek.org..

The People Who Change Your Life and Never Even Know It

by Kaitlin McCann
College of New Jersey Circle K

When I was little, I had everything I ever wanted or needed: a loving family, caring teachers and amazing friends. I was healthy and never thought that other people would have experiences that were different than my own.

Many years later, when I entered high school, I was faced with the decision of which clubs and organizations I would join. My best friend Beth told me that she was going to the Key Club meeting on Monday. I decided to tag along, although I did not know a great deal about the club or exactly what they did. Now, years later, I

For more information on Circle K, The Six Cents Initiative, or the Tomorrow Fund, please visit www.circlek.org.

know that this one decision changed my life and my interactions with others a great deal. It is often difficult to imagine how the decisions you make will influence your life and the people around you. However, I did not truly understand just how important of a decision this was until my second year in the club.

When I was a sophomore in high school, I was invited to attend a picnic that another Key Club was hosting. Initially, I was not sure if I would attend. However, when I arrived and heard that one of the Backstreet Boys would be attending, I was instantly excited about my decision. The picnic was a chance for children with disabilities and their parents to have a fun day in the park and participate in activities including games, competitions and arts and crafts. I was stationed at one of the arts and crafts tables where the children would make bracelets. I was excited but also skeptical; how could children with disabilities handle the small pieces needed to create these bracelets.

I waited around at the table for a long time, but no children came. Finally, a little girl named Jennifer came to my table. She was very excited to make a bracelet and I was very excited to help her. Little did I know that what would happen in those ten short minutes I spent with Jennifer would change me and my life forever. Jennifer suffered from a birth defect which left one of her hands crippled. It was very hard for her to hold anything, especially the small string she needed to put beads on to create her bracelet. However, Jennifer did not let that stop her. She worked very, very hard to find just the right beads and then began to thread them onto the string. I was amazed at how determined Jennifer was. Although the string moved and was hard to hold Jennifer struggled, but continued. She had lined up eight beads, a lofty task for her. However, after a matter of minutes I finally saw the finished product. The bracelet containing the eight beads arranged in order

"J-E-N-N-I-F-E-R".

For more information on Circle K, The Six Cents Initiative, or the Tomorrow Fund, please visit www.circlek.org..

For someone so small to have such great determination was inspiring. I had never had to face such a challenge as a child, but I imagined it could not be easy to go through life a little different than everyone else, but continue to be ambitious, excited and inspired to live each day. Jennifer lived her life the way I aspired to live mine and truly showed me what it means to work hard and overcome any challenge placed in your way.

Now, let's fast forward to the spring of my senior year of high school. I had been invited to attend a Circle K event with Richard Stockton College and was very excited to drive down and begin doing service with real college students. When I arrived at RSC, I was asked to attend a soup kitchen in Atlantic City. Once at the soup kitchen, my group was given the quick tour of the facilities and then put to work. After serving dinner to roughly one hundred people, one man came up to me and asked what I had done wrong to be forced to serve dinner here. Was I a community service worker? Had I committed a crime? I explained to him that, no, I had not been forced to come here. Instead, I had volunteered. He was amazed. He called me an angel for being willing to give of my time to help him and the other people at the soup kitchen. It was at that moment that I realized not everyone does community service. Helping others, although a part of my everyday life, was something that not all people did. This, for me was a real wake up call. It reminded me that no matter where life takes me or what I am doing, I must always have a heart of service. There are people just like me who need help and as long as I am able, I must continue to show others that there are people willing to help others just for the sheer purpose of helping.

Since these projects, I have traveled many places and met many people. I have served in various leadership positions and done numerous service projects. Each has impacted me in a different, yet inspiring way. However, what I have learned from all of this is that when you help others, you inevitably enrich your own life as well. When running for international office during my junior year of college, my friend Terry D. Williams asked me a question in one of the caucus rooms. His question was "Which statement is more true- Kaitlin McCann is better because of Circle K or Circle K is better because of Kaitlin McCann?"

For me, this was initially a difficult question. However, the answer for me was quite apparent. I am a better person because of my participation in Circle K and my interaction with all levels of the Kiwanis family. Despite all of the time and effort I have given to CKI, it cannot ever compare to all I have received in return. My challenge to you is this: each day when you wake up make the decision to be a servant leader. Remember all those people who you have touched and who have touched you. And last, at the end of each day, ask yourself if you have become a better person that day because of the interactions you have had. I hope that we can all continue to be leaders, humble servants and show the determination that Jennifer showed me that spring day more than six years ago.

People of Inspiration

by Amanda Lawing Sosebee
University of North Carolina at Greensboro Circle K

Camp Friendship is a camp for kids who have or have had Cancer and their siblings. This is my second year as a counselor, and my Circle K club sponsors a child to come to camp each year. I'm sitting at the "dance of the decades" watching Aaron, a former camper who has returned as a counselor. His brother, a Cancer Survivor, can't come to camp anymore because his family moved too far away. Still, Aaron returns each year to be with other survivors and, more importantly, children who are going through treatment right now. As he smiles, laughs, and encourages the shy little boys to dance, he knows that his experiences, and those of other campers, help those patients and their siblings get through the treatments. Camp gives them something to look forward to all year.

Lauren tells me that we met years ago going to Key Club International Convention, but I don't remember that. I remember going to our first District Large Scale Service Project and getting knocked over in a brutal game of Twister. I also remember her enthusiasm for painting the largest one-story building I've ever seen, knowing that it would help support the Boys and Girls Home. Since then, I've seen her organize events and conventions, earn national grants, own other players in Apples to Apples, and help put this book together, all without the slightest sign of stress. More importantly, though, I've heard her stories of helping others and changing lives.

Nicole never meant to get so involved. She came to our club's Circle K meeting enthusiastic to help people and interested in learning more. She left a few weeks later as a member of the first Empty Bowls Student Planning Committee. She didn't know about the hours of planning she would have to do, or the endless contacts she would have to make. She did know that she would be impacting our campus and community and improving the lives of the patrons of our local homeless shelter. Despite all of the extra, unexpected work, she still signed up for even more work when she helped plan an International Festival at the local Boys and Girls Club. Through all of the obstacles she faced, she always found a way to make things work. She probably didn't mean to, but she inspired countless others to help our campus and community, too.

For more information on Circle K, The Six Cents Initiative, or the Tomorrow Fund, please visit www.circlek.org..

Mike is the best person I know at reading people. He goes to the Large Scale Service Project excited about meeting new people. Throughout the week, he'll sit down and have conversations with the majority of the people there. During the conversation, he uses his special gift for making people feel welcome and important. He notices when someone sits away from the rest of the group, and he makes sure to talk to them. By the end of a conversation, he has normally convinced them to come take part in the group activity. Over the rest of the project, he lets them know, often without saying it, that they are a valuable part of the group, and he means it every time.

All in all, Elisa was just a normal high school kid. She probably joined Key Club because her friends were doing it, and she wanted to fit in with the group. What set her apart was that she was willing to help other people fit in with the group, too. I joined Key Club because my mom, a former Kiwanian, recommended it. I usually sat by myself, and didn't socialize much at projects. Elisa encouraged me to spend more time with the group and to come to more events. If it weren't for her, I probably would not have stayed in Key Club, nor would I have joined Circle K. I hope she knows how her friendliness changed my life.

It took me a long time to figure out what inspires me to help others. I finally realized that what makes me want to change the world is seeing other people doing just that. Like Aaron, Lauren, Nicole, Mike, Elisa, and countless others have all had a lasting impact on my life, I know that, without even trying, I can do the same for others. Together, we are making the world a better place. That is what inspires me to make a difference.

For more information on Circle K, The Six Cents Initiative, or the Tomorrow Fund, please visit www.circlek.org.

For more information on Circle K, The Six Cents Initiative, or the Tomorrow Fund, please visit www.circlek.org..

SECTION II:
THE SPEECHES

The second part of this book is no less inspirational than the first, but these writings are designed to be speeches given to public audiences, typically on what Circle K is about. The three tenets of Circle K are Service, Leadership, and Fellowship, and so it becomes difficult to tell someone what Circle K is all about with only one story or example. The unspoken fact inherent in these speeches is that college students, who normally despise and even fear public speaking, have stood in front of audiences and delivered these speeches. In that alone, they are going beyond what most people expect, and hopefully you will find their words and bravery inspirational.

What is Circle K?

by Katy Giesken
Clemson University Circle K

I stand before you as a member of an amazing organization known as Circle K International. For some college students, Circle K is merely the next step in continuing their Kiwanis family career. For others, it is their first step into a world of service, leadership, and fellowship. But some may wonder "what exactly is Circle K?" Circle K provides college students with the opportunities to serve their communities, develop their skills as leaders, and meet fellow Circle Kers from other schools, districts, and around the world.

For more information on Circle K, The Six Cents Initiative, or the Tomorrow Fund, please visit www.circlek.org.

Circle K's service is vast and varied. It may take the form of members teaching children how to read. It may take the form of supporting allied organizations, such as Relay for Life, or UNICEF. Or it may take the form of 30 college students from two states coming together over a weekend to prime and paint a country store at the Boys and Girls Home at Lake Waccamaw. Whatever form the service takes, Circle K'ers dedicate their time and energy to changing the world one project at a time.

One of my favorite service projects has always been Trick-or-Treating for UNICEF. This past year, Clemson Circle K dressed up in various costumes and actually went trick-or-treating for change. Although this project seems to only be social and fun, it is in fact making a large difference in our world. A few years ago, all the money from Trick-or-Treating went to the UNICEF project to reduce the occurrences of iodine deficiency disorder in third world countries. Because of our efforts and those of other organizations and members of the Kiwanis Family, we were able to eliminate iodine deficiency disorder from the earth.

Another project that touched me personally was through my home club where I took part in the Clemson Elementary School Fall Carnival. All of our volunteers were involved in running the small games set up, painting faces, or working the food table. But not me. My job was to stay with a giant plywood elephant. After studying it for quite some time, I discovered that to work this elephant, I had to stand behind it and slide my arm through the sweater sleeve that went to the front and acted as the elephant's trunk. A child would walk up, hand the elephant's trunk their ticket, the elephant would "eat" the ticket through the flap mouth and pull out a small prize from the little basket of toys.

For more information on Circle K, The Six Cents Initiative, or the Tomorrow Fund, please visit www.circlek.org..

At the beginning of the day, some of the children seemed slightly afraid of the large elephant, but as the day went on the elephant quickly became one of the most popular attractions at the carnival. In fact there were several times where we had to tell the children that the elephant was asleep so that we would have enough time to get more prizes. I'll admit, I was slightly skeptical as I walked up to that elephant on that Fall morning. But as I walked away that afternoon, all I could do was smile to myself remembering all the smiles and laughter of the children I played with that day.

Another unique aspect of Circle K is the leadership opportunities. Circle K is structured to be lead by its student members, including an international president, vice-president and board of representatives; a district board, consisting of a Governor, a Secretary/Treasurer, a Bulletin Editor, and Lt. Governors; and then a club board, consisting of a president, vice president, secretary, and treasurer. Each of these positions is filled by election from the student members.

I currently serve as Lt. Governor of the Metro and Palmetto Divisions of the Carolinas District, where I counsel and help clubs reach the goals they set for themselves. This role has not only provided me with the opportunities to develop my leadership and communication skills, but it has also provided me with the knowledge necessary to possibly pursue other leadership positions in the future, both inside Circle K and after graduation. But Circle K is not one large competition to see who can complete the most services and rise to the top of the leadership ladder. The characteristic that truly sets Circle K apart from other organizations is the fellowship.

For more information on Circle K, The Six Cents Initiative, or the Tomorrow Fund, please visit www.circlek.org.

The easiest way to demonstrate this fellowship is to share a quick story with you. While I had always heard Circle K being referred to as a part of the Kiwanis Family, I had never experienced the intense, family-like bond until I attended the Kiwanis Family Conference in October 2006. This was the first international event I attended where Kiwanians, Circle Kers, and Key Clubbers all participated as equals.

Although the weekend was filled with laughter and friendly competition, it is the serious part of that weekend that I will never forget. I found myself sitting in a circle in a pitch black room with my small family for the weekend answering boundary breaking questions. A boundary breaking question is one in which you have to delve deep into yourself to find an answer. The only way to benefit from boundary breaking questions to be completely honest with yourself and those around you. Because of the bonds, closeness, and genuine caring that the Kiwanis family provides, I found myself able to share thoughts and ideas that even my closest friends do not know. I may never remember the questions that night, or the answers that I gave, or even the names of the people in the circle who I could no longer see. However, I will never forget the feeling of fellowship, family, and trust that existed in that room.

Circle K International is world-wide collegiate service organization dedicated to bettering the world, our communities, and the lives of children. However, it sets itself apart by making its members part of a family. And I want to thank you for being a part of that family.

(First delivered at Carolina Kiwanis District Convention, Hilton Head Island, SC in August of 2007)

For more information on Circle K, The Six Cents Initiative, or the Tomorrow Fund, please visit www.circlek.org..

A Foundation of Service

by Ashley Hedges
University of North Carolina at Chapel Hill Circle K

Circle K International is a student-run organization consisting of college students, defined as a group of responsible leaders with a lifelong commitment to volunteering and bettering the community worldwide. The three pillars of Circle K – service, leadership, and fellowship – shape individual members of this club to become active, contributing citizens, dedicated to making the world a better place.

For more information on Circle K, The Six Cents Initiative, or the Tomorrow Fund, please visit www.circlek.org.

As one of the main tenets of Circle K, service forms the foundation on which the club stands. Each year, Circle K members contribute more than one million service hours to their communities, both small and large. From renovating buildings, to raising funds for AIDS and cancer awareness, to promoting education and tutoring programs, Circle K has an impact on almost every member of our community. Circle Kers also place an emphasis on serving the children of the world, by promoting literacy campaigns and contributing to the Boys and Girls Home annually.

Circle Kers put an unimaginable amount of work and dedication to service, and through it all, they develop as strong, confident leaders within our community; thus, leadership serves as the second tenet of this organization. Circle K offers a variety of active roles and training conferences that help shape them into successful leaders, all aimed at the goal of empowering members to realize their full potential and accomplish tasks even they may have thought unobtainable.

Circle K members are not unaccustomed to accomplishing larger goals through the strength of team work. I can think of one example in my freshman year of college that motivated me to become dedicated to this extraordinary club. The project was the first District Large Scale Service Project of the year, and it included a trip to the Boys and Girls Home, a program dedicated to renewing hope and rebuilding the lives of children and families.

That weekend, our group of Circle Kers was put in charge of painting a country store at the Boys and Girls Home, since it was one of their major sources of income for their program. The building was large and the project seemed impossible to accomplish in just two short days, but the members of Circle K each picked up a brush and set to work. It was powerful to see so many students from different universities all working together for a common goal. Yes, even Carolina and Duke were working side-by-side.

Here were a group of college kids, who probably had so many other things on their plate, giving up their weekend to travel to a small community just to put in a few hours of volunteer work. Yet the thirty students that showed up that weekend accomplished so much, and through that shared experience created a bond built on laughter and hard work. You never realize how much you have in common with people so different from you until you join together with them on a task that maybe even you might have thought was impossible at first glance.

The bonds formed that weekend are a synonymous component of all Circle K events, as fellowship stands as the third and final pillar of this organization. Whether members are planning a local fundraiser, collecting books for children in Africa, or interacting with senior citizens, Circle Kers always take the time to welcome new people. Circle Kers develop communication skills, but more importantly they develop lifelong friendships.

The members of Circle K are the most important component of the organization, because without active members, there is nothing to ensure the continued success of this program. Circle K is always looking to recruit more students, to encourage them to contribute to their dedication to the betterment of mankind. So if you find you may be even a little interested in Circle K, I would encourage you to check out their website at circlek.org, or to check for local clubs within universities across the globe, because with the friendships you form and the experiences you gain, you may just find yourself changing the world.

For more information on Circle K, The Six Cents Initiative, or the Tomorrow Fund, please visit www.circlek.org.

For more information on Circle K, The Six Cents Initiative, or the Tomorrow Fund,
please visit www.circlek.org..

Service+Leadership+Fellowship=K-Love

by Nicholas Evans
North Carolina State University Circle K

My first event with Circle K, I learned just what the organization is all about. The event was Kiwanis Family Conference held in beautiful Black Mountain North Carolina which I have attended for the past 5 years, 4 of which were with Key Club. It was evident as soon as I walked in the room that fateful day that this group of individuals was going to change who I was. It wasn't even a sanctioned Circle K event, but right there and then, I learned exactly what K-Love is all about. The three tenets of Circle K are lived every day, in every member, in every college throughout the country and beyond where a club exists.

For more information on Circle K, The Six Cents Initiative, or the Tomorrow Fund, please visit www.circlek.org.

Through service, leadership, and fellowship, one big family is created with all the right ideals necessary for changing the world and making a difference. It's not just another college campus organization, but an honest to God way of life.

So you may all think that I'm just a bright and goofy individual. I can promise I haven't always been like this. What you see standing before you was Circle K's doing. With all of the crazy events that are so fun and so group oriented, I learned quickly that I couldn't just sit back and watch everyone like I used to do. I actually had to break out of my shell that I was in all throughout middle and high school, and get to know everyone that I could because I had been having so much fun with all of them. I'll tell you right now, if I had the opportunity to go back in time and change everything about this past year, I wouldn't change a single thing to do with Circle K.

Over the course of this past year, I've taken part in my different community service activities ranging from large to small, from local to school and even local for home which is a good three and half hour drive from school. I have to say that my favorite opportunity for service as of yet this year has to be DLSSP at the Boys and Girls Homes of NC at Lake Waccamaw, simply because it's such an inviting atmosphere, and there is so much to do to help the individuals that live at the Home. Doing work at the Home is so rewarding because you know that you're actually making a difference. We have the privilege of meeting the kids and teens that live there, and we get to interact with them, which is something that you aren't offered in most situations.

For more information on Circle K, The Six Cents Initiative, or the Tomorrow Fund, please visit www.circlek.org..

During my years in Key Club, I had plenty of chances to gain leadership experience, and I'm sure that I did. But I was never motivated enough to hold a leadership position. However, after my first year of involvement with Circle K, I was motivated enough to do so because of the individuals I had met and because of what I had seen my friends accomplish in the club. Even without holding a position on the district board, I feel as though I will gain much in terms of leadership skills than my previous experiences in Key Club. With Circle K, there are so many opportunities to enhance your leadership skills such as group activities, boundary breaking, and committees. I've found my place in the K-family again, and I couldn't be happier.

Fellowship. What is there to say about it? It's an idea, a notion conceived by a group of individuals who have a common purpose, but it's still so much more than that. Fellowship is love, honesty, compassion, and any other inspirational word you could possibly use to describe something positive. I've found fellowship here in Circle K. I've made more new friends in this organization within the past year than I have in probably my entire high school career. It's simply amazing how people this caring can get to you and make a home in your heart so warm, it's like there's a fireplace there that never stops burning.

Through all of the events, friends, and service opportunities, I've learned what Circle K means to me. It's more than just another organization which you can provide service to the local and extended community. Circle K is a family and much more. Through the tenets of service, leadership, and fellowship, every individual of the organization has the chance and the ability to better themselves.

For more information on Circle K, The Six Cents Initiative, or the Tomorrow Fund,
please visit www.circlek.org..

Discovering Myself in Circle K

by Anita Iari

Clemson University Circle K

Archimedes was quoted as saying, "Give me a lever long enough and a fulcrum on which to place it and I shall move the world." As much as I would have loved to tell you three years ago that I would move the world if you handed me a really long lever with a fulcrum, I probably would have stood there holding the two objects in my hand staring at you with a confused look on my face. Yes, I have been ambitious my whole life, however, there is only so far that ambition can take a person without any life-long skills.

For more information on Circle K, The Six Cents Initiative, or the Tomorrow Fund, please visit www.circlek.org.

Circle K's three tenets have honestly found a true place in my heart. If you would have told me three years ago to do community service, I would have asked you what I did wrong. However, being a member of Circle K has shown me that service isn't about being forced to do work due to doing something wrong. Instead, service is about Circle K members coming together as one to serve the world in need.

Seeing the difference we make is what motivates us as an organization to do more, change more, fix more. As Circle K Clubs from all over North and South Carolina join together at Lake Waccamaw, a sense of passion and motivation is felt in the air as members gather at the Boys and Girls Home excitedly awaiting to hear the projects needed to be done for the upcoming weekend.

Once the projects were assigned, members wasted no time in spreading out to different rooms of the Kiwanis Cottage to begin painting, going outside to rake and power wash, as well as head over to the field to pick up sticks. After painting and bonding with people for a couple of hours, I took a break and walked around the Kiwanis Cottage. I remembered the last time we were here, just last semester. About 30 Circle K'ers with the same goal of making the Kiwanis Cottage better through serving the Boys and Girls Home.

I remember walking through the back door, all the rooms completely bare. There was a mission put in front of us, and we worked together to accomplish it, painting side by side as well as sharing conversations full of hopes for our future. I walked through the doors again to see what the rooms looked like since we have painted them. My mouth almost dropped to the floor when I walked into the one bedroom we painted and I saw a bed and dressers. A quick flashback reminded me of what that room had looked like a couple months ago, empty except for the ladders that members were standing on with their brushes, paint, and huge smiles on their faces.

For more information on Circle K, The Six Cents Initiative, or the Tomorrow Fund, please visit www.circlek.org..

I excitedly ran into the living room and saw two couches, a coffee table, and a TV. At this point my heart filled with joy and I couldn't help but let a huge smile take over my face. Did we really do this? Was this really the same empty room that numerous students had filled at one time? It looked like an actual home, and if it provided a home to somebody, then we as the Carolinas District had accomplished our mission. We may not have realized it as much at the time, but looking at now, I can't believe we are the ones that worked together to make a home for somebody.

Anybody who provides service like this to a community is considered a leader in Circle K. Taking a step above and beyond is what defines a Circle K member. We are not afraid to step up and do what is needed to help serve the world around us. On top of being leaders of our community through service, we are also given the chance of taking on other leadership positions on numerous levels of the organization.

Never experiencing a leadership position in my life before Circle K, I was a little hesitant in raising my hand to run for club treasurer my freshman year. Although I didn't end up winning the position, there was somebody in the room who had confidence in me. He nominated me for Club Secretary, and it was definitely a role that has changed my life as a leader, especially after attending Club Officer Training that year. I got into a group with the rest of the secretaries at one point during that weekend, and sat down with a facilitator to listen to our roles as secretaries.

"Being secretary, you hold the most important position on your club board." I looked around to make sure I was with the right group of people. Yes, those were secretaries surrounding me left and right. MOST IMPORTNANT POSITION?!?

OK, just breathe Anita, was all I could say to myself. Although towards the beginning of the weekend I had been feeling scared to speak up about my ideas, by the end, I could not stop talking. Through several team building activities as well as learning how to set SMART goals, motivation had hit me hard on my head. I began to realize that it was actually OK for me to dream big and share my ideas to help better this organization. This experience has changed my life by helping me become more confident in my abilities as a leader as well as have faith in myself to lead a district to keep striving toward greatness.

As motivated Circle K members, it should be no surprise that we strive to serve our communities as positive role models and leaders. However, Circle K has one more tenet that has made a huge difference in my life.—Fellowship.

Coming to the South for school from New Jersey was a sensitive time in my life. It was the first time I was leaving my family, my support system 12 hours behind to start off on a new foot as an independent adult for the first time in my life. As excited as I was, I was also completely clueless once my father had left me behind.

However, I speak from my heart when I say that Circle K has honestly helped shape me into the person I am today. Not only through service and leadership experiences, but also by giving me a support system. I met numerous people who I honestly consider family, people who I know I can call in my times in need, people who are willing to help whenever and wherever. And I truly mean WHENEVER and WHEREVER.

How many people are willing to drive you to a national park at 6 in the morning to help look for your car keys. I had initially felt so stupid for losing my keys in the first place as well as horrible for making somebody go out with me that early in the morning to a HUGE PARK to look for my keys. After they were found in the middle of a bunch of trees, Jeffrey Marsocci took me out for breakfast at Bojangles. I wanted to pay to show him my appreciation, but he wouldn't let me touch my wallet.

That morning, we bonded, and I realized that he wasn't angry or upset with me, and he didn't look down on me. I felt that it was all OK, and these were people that were willing to help me, rather than scold me. I felt like I had finally found the support I needed and people like Jeff as well as numerous others have supported me throughout my years in college. Supported me in times of stress and believed in me when other haven't.

Circle K has helped me become a person I am proud to be today. I look back at my freshman year of college and I still see myself as a confused little girl trying to find my place in the world. And I finally have. I finally found a way to share my passion of helping others with other Circle K members. I have learned to stand up strong and fight for what I believe in. And lastly, I have found a family away from home that has helped me in more ways than I can ever express. People that have helped me believe in myself for the first time in my life, and there is nothing I can be more thankful for.

For more information on Circle K, The Six Cents Initiative, or the Tomorrow Fund, please visit www.circlek.org.

For more information on Circle K, The Six Cents Initiative, or the Tomorrow Fund, please visit www.circlek.org..

Making a Difference in Life

by Lauren Burianek
University of North Carolina at Chapel Hill Circle K

Caring. Passion. Love. Excitement. Service. Leadership. Family. What do all of these words have in common? Sure, they all create a warm fuzzy feeling, and they all might make you smile. But what they REALLY all have in common is that they all represent the wonderful organization of Circle K. Let me tell you something…you really do attain lifelong friends pumping gas all day…(pause) I'm just kidding! But really, Circle K International is the largest student-led collegiate service organization in the world, and that's nothing to scoff at. By uniting college students together under one cause, Circle K shows that one CAN make a difference, but in a team full of people, they can change the world. It enables

For more information on Circle K, The Six Cents Initiative, or the Tomorrow Fund, please visit www.circlek.org.

college students to provide service to the world around them, follow their passions, and take others to new heights.

When I first got involved in the Kiwanis family, it was just another thing to add to the resume, another experience not unlike every position I had held before. However, it wasn't long before I was proved wrong. It wasn't long before I was immersed in a world full of engaging events, meeting new people, actively participating in service projects, and even dressing up in Halloween costumes in the middle of May to raise money for children in Africa. It wasn't long before I realized that this organization was my new family, my new dedication, and my new passion. I wanted to do everything I could to get involved and make a difference, and the Kiwanis family allowed me to do that.

The great thing about Circle K is that it is more than just a club – it has a District level, a regional level, and an international level, allowing students to get as involved as they wish. If they like planning events and motivating others, then they have the opportunity to be on the District Board. If they like the behind the scenes paperwork and organization, then they can run for a Secretary or Treasurer position within the club. Or, if they would simply rather do hands on service, then being an active member is right for them. Regardless, Circle K can offer positions for any need – and more. But it doesn't just offer positions and something to put on a resume. It offers the resources, skills, and training required to not only allow students to excel in personal development, but also allow them to turn around and teach those same skills to people around them, resulting in a leadership cascade of young adults trying to make a difference in the world around them.

For more information on Circle K, The Six Cents Initiative, or the Tomorrow Fund, please visit www.circlek.org..

There's more to just leadership, however… there's what *makes* a student want to take on a leadership role – a sense of family…a passion for being with their best friends and the people that will always be there for them no matter what. Someone once told me a story about her wedding…half of her family couldn't make it, but her Circle K friends from over a decade back were willing to drive across the country just to be there for the ceremony. That's what some may call fellowship…but personally, that's what I call family.

Last but not least, there is what brings that family together under one roof – the delight of service, of helping others, of putting a smile on someone's face or a tear of happiness in their eyes. Service isn't just something we do – it's a lifestyle. It's what drives every aspect of our lives. In this world full of greed and gluttony, we are full of hope and inspiration. In this world full of pessimism and negativity, we see the glass half full. In this world full of hunger and hurt, we want to make a difference. We've been told that ONE can make a difference. And one CAN make a difference. But together, united under one cause, under one passion, and under one family…we can contribute so much more.

That's what Circle K is about…contributing so much more, not only to society, but to the students themselves and to the outside world.

For more information on Circle K, The Six Cents Initiative, or the Tomorrow Fund, please visit www.circlek.org..

Leaving A Mark on the World

by Jacqui Moskel

University of North Carolina at Chapel Hill Circle K

Webster's Dictionary defines service as the "contribution to the welfare of others." To Circle Kers service is much more; it incorporates fellowship and leadership to make simple, ordinary service projects into memorable moments that have an everlasting affect on the communities they touch.

For more information on Circle K, The Six Cents Initiative, or the Tomorrow Fund, please visit www.circlek.org.

Service is the foundation of Circle K. Unlike most other service organizations found on college campuses, Circle K clubs do not just focus on one specific project or even one realm of their community. Instead, the organization allows individual clubs and members to take on service projects that specifically interest them; students can do work for the homeless, the elderly, and schoolchildren all within a single club environment. UNC-CH is an example of such a club that exemplifies the diversity Circle K has to offer. UNC members have the opportunity to volunteer at the children's hospital on campus, at the Ronald McDonald house, at a local retirement home, and participate in fundraising walks such as March of Dimes and Relay for Life, to name just a few of their various activities.

While service is at the core of Circle K, the leadership members provide sustains the organization. The great Circle K leaders are those that work to find and bring out the leaders in everybody. I speak from experience, when I say that it is an amazing feeling to help a fellow Circle Ker realize their own leadership potential and take on more leadership responsibility at either the club or district level and then watch them grow and succeed beyond their expectations. Circle K has the great ability to not just focus on making officers effective leaders, but helps to ensure that a leader is found in every member.

Fellowship is the heart of Circle K. Circle Kers are brought together through the passion of service. With such a strong commonality to bond over there is little wondering to how we become the best of friends, a family away from home.

For more information on Circle K, The Six Cents Initiative, or the Tomorrow Fund, please visit www.circlek.org..

The event that demonstrates the three tenants of Circle K— service, leadership, and fellowship—to their full capacity is the Carolinas' District Large Scale Service Project, also known as DLSSP. The event, held twice a year, brings anywhere from 30 to 50 Circle Kers from schools all throughout the Carolinas together to do various projects at the Boys and Girls Home at Lake Waccamaw. I am always amazed at the dedication that is brought by every member to the projects and how quickly friendships are created. Throughout the weekend we work as one. School rivalries dissipated and we come together as a family. If it was not for the teamwork and motivation that we can create and bring to this project, we would not be able to accomplish nearly as much as we do during each weekend.

Circle K is an international organization that strives to connect Circle Kers from diverse backgrounds and schools under the umbrella of service. We are brought together through service, leadership, and fellowship to grow and create an everlasting mark on the world.

For more information on Circle K, The Six Cents Initiative, or the Tomorrow Fund, please visit www.circlek.org.

For more information on Circle K, The Six Cents Initiative, or the Tomorrow Fund,
please visit www.circlek.org..

An Organization That Knows No Limits

by Stephanie Northcott
University of North Carolina at Greensboro Circle K

When most people think of the word "service," usually think "Oh, I don't have time for that. I'm way too busy." Circle Kers do not even know how to utter that sentence. Service in their thing, and helping others is their game. With the three aspects of Circle K being leadership, fellowship, and service, this organization knows no limits.

For more information on Circle K, The Six Cents Initiative, or the Tomorrow Fund, please visit www.circlek.org.

Circle K offers an abundance of leadership roles and better prepares you for life in general. Through trainings, icebreakers, and leadership-oriented games you can develop a better sense of learning to lead and follow. I have only been a part of Circle K for four months, and already I have become a lieutenant governor of the Carolinas District.

While I walked into the situation thinking, "Oh my gosh! I have no clue what I'm doing!" I quickly learned that there were friendly faces pushing me in the right directions, towards the right resources, and helping me discover that leadership is nothing to be afraid of. Yes, there will be times when solutions seem unattainable, but there are people available to encourage you and give you confidence to find your way.

Leadership roles in Circle K are like waves in the ocean. Just like an ocean wouldn't be an ocean without waves, Circle K would not be Circle K without leadership opportunities. There are tons of ways to be involved in Circle K International, and all you have to do is open your eyes to find them.

For about five years now I have been involved in the Kiwanis family and I have made some of the best friendship I have ever known. One of my favorite things about the Carolinas District is our District Events. While we do attend to business, Service is the focus of Circle K International. Through service, members learn to come together to achieve a common goal and better the lives of others. At the Spring District Large Scale Service Project thirty-four members of Circle K from all across the Carolinas gathered in the small, quaint town of Lake Waccamaw.

This small group of people performed service tasks throughout the weekend to better the Boys and Girls Home. "So, I guess ya'll can start on this old theatre room and just gut it out," said Mr. Hewitt as we began to form groups of cleanup crews to tackle the mission. "It should take you all day to finish."

Members came together and completely emptied the room top to bottom, all before lunch. If that wasn't amazing, after we downed a few hot dogs, we completed a project that was expected to take at least four hours more. Together, as a whole, no longer individuals, we bonded to complete the task at hand.

Jane Doe

by Kathleen Marsocci
Kiwanis Young Professionals of Raleigh

Good evening and thank you for being here. Tonight, we gather together to spotlight the sponsored leadership programs of the Carolinas District, including Circle K. Unfortunately, our Circle K Governor Kathryn Geiger is not able to address you this evening. She just finished up a summer internship in New Jersey at 5 o'clock this evening, but even with a little bending of the speed limits, we were fairly certain that she would not be able to drive here in time to be with us this evening.

For more information on Circle K, The Six Cents Initiative, or the Tomorrow Fund, please visit www.circlek.org.

As a new Circle K Administrator taking over in the middle of the sponsored youth year, I have had the privilege to work with two outstanding district boards over the last 10 months. As a past Circle K governor myself, I had my own view of Kiwanis. As a Kiwanian now viewing Circle K from the other side of the relationship, I truly feel that Circle K members are college-aged Kiwanians, serving their communities and campuses with the same energy, caring and enthusiasm as our own Kiwanis clubs.

While I received a lot of support from our Kiwanis district when I took over as administrator, I feel that I received most of my on the job training (really, more of a trial by fire) from last year's Circle K district board. I am happy to report that some of last year's Circle K district board members who relinquished their membership in Circle K at the conclusion of their International Convention just last week are now in the process of applying for membership in Kiwanis Clubs in the Carolinas.

I could tell you about all of the fantastic things that Circle K is doing in the Carolinas, but we have a lot of that information at our table outside and we'll see it in a slide show in a few minutes. I could tell you what Circle K means to me, but that will better come from one of the Circle K district board members, who will address you in just a few moments. Instead, I would like to tell you about what Kiwanis meant to a former Circle K member.

Jane Doe, which is not her real name, grew up under adverse conditions, to say the least. As the oldest child, it was often her responsibility to care for the other children in the house. Her mother was always at work, and her father was usually intoxicated, and she often had to be the one to drive and pick him up because he was not able to make it home on his own. Throughout all of her personal trials at home, Jane flourished in school. One of the main reasons she did so well was because in high school she was in Key

Club and had a truly inspiring and involved sponsoring Kiwanis Club she could look up to.

Jane's Kiwanis role models knew nothing of her home life. They had no idea that when Jane attended their weekly meetings they were often treating her to her only hot meal that week. They had no idea how their small words of encouragement often kept Jane going another week when all she wanted to do was give up and hide. They had no idea how just the example of Kiwanians in Jane's life kept her on the right track, how she received a full scholarship to college and eventually graduated with honors. Or how their civic involvement inspired Jane to join Circle K at her college and become one of their most dedicated leaders. Her sponsoring Kiwanis Club never knew how Jane's life was impacted by the little things they did to help her and inspire her.

While Jane's sponsoring Kiwanis Club had no idea how they were impacting her life at the time, she has since told them her story. They now have also seen how she has impacted Circle K, stepping forward time and again as a leader, and how she has gone on to Grad School, and how she will likely be in a Kiwanis Club once she graduates. Through a few simple acts of kindness, a child grew up through extremely difficult circumstances to serve others.

How many children have been affected by Jane's efforts in Circle K? How many can tabs have been donated to the Ronald McDonald House because of her organizational skills? How many nursing home patients have been given a smile because Jane was there? How many elementary school children have seen Jane and her fellow Circle K members help them, and then decided that they too had the strength and drive and determination to make our world a better place?

Thank you Kiwanians of the Carolinas District for your support of Circle K, for your support of all of our sponsored leadership programs, and especially for all that you do for the Janes of our world.

(First delivered at Carolina Kiwanis District Convention, Hilton Head Island, SC in August of 2007)

For more information on Circle K, The Six Cents Initiative, or the Tomorrow Fund, please visit www.circlek.org..

What is Normal?

by Melissa Summer
Furman University Circle K

Albert Einstein once said, "Only a life lived for others is a life worthwhile." As a life-long Girl Scout, serving others is my passion. I worried how I would maintain this life mission in college. Actually, for the first few weeks of freedom from home, I decided to be normal for a change. I refused to be a leader. I refused to brainstorm and initiate service projects. In fact, I refused to attend meetings and projects associated with Circle K, a student-led service organization I discovered at our fall activities

For more information on Circle K, The Six Cents Initiative, or the Tomorrow Fund, please visit www.circlek.org.

fair. Passions, however, do not give in easily. That's how I fell helplessly in love with Circle K and its three tenants: service, leadership, and fellowship. It's been a crazy adventure since I gave up on my short-lived dream of being "normal."

Service to others largely defines my life. During my freshman year—remember that "normal" phase I went through?—my friends kept a tally on our refrigerator of the "number of whales" I'd "saved." I thought the community service I performed was normal, but apparently my relentless dedication to volunteering was not. I didn't mind—Circle K accepted my obsession with "saving whales" with open arms.

I participate in group projects with Hope Chest, a local retail store supporting battered women. We care for disadvantaged children at A Child's Haven while their parents attended a parenting class. We help with the Special Olympics hosted at Furman. We support Furman's annual May Day Play Day, a student-organized, themed-activity day for community children. We chaperone children through dorms for trick-or-treating. I help with pet therapy at the Washington Center, which benefits children with disabilities. We donate cards and blankets to the local children's hospital.

Most recently, our club raised $500 for the Six Cents Initiative on campus. Six cents purchases an oral rehydration packet for children in countries lacking water purification systems. We saved over 8,330 lives. Last week, we kicked off a hat collection drive for patients undergoing chemotherapy. In a couple of weeks, we will also be hosting our first independent service project on a larger scale—we will invite children to a Saturday Matinee, where they will enjoy games, snacks, crafts and a card-making service project, and a movie. The charitable donations from their parents will mostly benefit A Child's Haven.

For more information on Circle K, The Six Cents Initiative, or the Tomorrow Fund, please visit www.circlek.org..

All of these activities are only within our club. As an entire district, we support the Boys and Girls' Club in Lake Waccamaw, North Carolina. We have renovated buildings, provided food for their horses for a year by clearing sticks out of the field, and showed an impressionable group that Circle K cares. A quote that particularly defines Circle K members' dedication to service is: "You cannot do all the good the world needs, but the world needs all the good you can do."

Of course, service is not free-standing—leadership inevitably surfaces. Remember how I strove to be normal and avoided Circle K like the plague? Well, I ended up serving as treasurer at the end of my freshman year. That wasn't leadership, though—not in my mind. That was merely playing with other people's money, and I liked math.

Once again, Circle K continued to follow me. Six months later, I found myself grappling with the realization that I had been asked to run for president. I was quite hesitant. What happened to my "normal" life? Finally, I realized maybe I was destined *not* to be normal—or at least not "normal" in *my* idea of the word. Perhaps normal was serving in a leadership capacity. Perhaps normal was guiding others to discover their potential. Perhaps normal was serving as president of Furman's Circle K for a year and a half so that we could re-align ourselves with the district calendar. Perhaps normal was re-building our club after struggling for three years after we were chartered.

The dream of being normal—as in the traditional, non-Melissian sense of the word—always remained tucked in the back of my brain. When I announced a few months ago that I would not run for a position on our club board to allow others' leadership skills to blossom, I thought I could finally attain that sense of college-kid normalcy I'd dreamed of for so long.

For more information on Circle K, The Six Cents Initiative, or the Tomorrow Fund, please visit www.circlek.org.

Walking back to my apartment after that announcement, however, I my heavy heart felt empty. I was confused. Then I realized—Circle K had become my sense of normal. Being out of a leadership role in Circle K was *not* normal. That night, I submitted an application to serve as the Lieutenant Governor of the Palmetto Division of Circle K. Here I stand. Apparently, I can do no other. Circle K sees the talents we sometimes don't see or refuse to see. I am a leader because of Circle K.

Though service and leadership are great, we can't forget the importance of fellowship. Ask any Circle K member about the friends they've met through this organization, and you will likely hear all about their family away from home. What else would you expect from members of a group who unite to serve, lead, and change the world?

I love the extremely diverse backgrounds of our Furman Circle K members. Almost every single one of us has a different major, and therefore we bring many different strengths, interests, and resources to make our family even stronger. We're serious about service, but we're also serious about having fun. I must admit I was terrified to attend my first district convention last year in Burlington. I was the only Furman representative, and I worried I would be lost without my well-loved Circle K family. Instead, I found a more extensive family with members from colleges and universities across the Carolinas.

I saw first-hand the passion we all shared and our unquestioned dedication to making a difference. I couldn't wait for DCON this year so I could see all my Circle K friends from other schools as well as meet new friends. Now that I'm on the district board, I've discovered a new level of fellowship, friendship, and family. Crazy times—that's about all I have to say. Oh, and that we all love cheesecake.

For more information on Circle K, The Six Cents Initiative, or the Tomorrow Fund, please visit www.circlek.org..

Einstein was right—it's all relative. I may not be "normal" in the traditional sense of the word, but in Circle K, I am normal. I can share my passion for service and leadership with a family just as normal as me. I can share my vision of making a difference without being ridiculed—in fact, I might even find some enthusiastic whale-savers willing to join me. Through service, leadership, and fellowship, Circle K empowers me to work with other college students and Kiwanis members to change the world, one life at a time.

For more information on Circle K, The Six Cents Initiative, or the Tomorrow Fund, please visit www.circlek.org.

The Opportunity to Serve

by Susan Shmania

University of North Carolina at Chapel Hill Circle K

Circle K is the college level of Kiwanis, an international community service organization that is dedicated to improving the lives of children. The three tenants of Circle K are: service, leadership, and fellowship. I have been an active volunteer in my community since the beginning of high school and when I started at Carolina I began to look for ways to become more involved on campus and to volunteer in the local community.

For more information on Circle K, The Six Cents Initiative, or the Tomorrow Fund, please visit www.circlek.org.

I began my involvement in Circle K with the idea that the organization would simply serve as a way for me to continue to find volunteer service opportunities in the area. I chose to become involved with Circle K, rather than another organization, because I had been a member of Key Club in high school and I was somewhat familiar with the Kiwanis Family.

Dust was everywhere. There were old computers—some working, some not—in piles on the floor. There were tables, desks, and even a piano and an old, broken tanning machine. It was the 2007 Spring District Large Scale Service Project (DLSSP), my first district event. It was also the first time I began to understand the true significance of our work.

We began the day with a large storage room full of old computers, furniture, and other objects. By the middle of the afternoon we had cleaned out the room, taken the computers and furniture to the Country Store, ripped up the old carpeting, and even washed the walls. We finished the task after only several hours of concentrated work. In fact, we were so ahead of schedule that they had to find new projects for us to do before we finished for the day. Because of our work, the Boys and Girls Home was able to use the newly cleared space in order to expand their offices for both foster care and adoption services. The task only took us a few hours of effort, but the work that we did has allowed the Boys and Girls Home to improve their job of helping improve the lives of children in need.

My experience at this DLSSP inspired me to apply for the leadership position of District Service Project Committee Chair this year. Leadership is another of the tenants of Circle K. As well as club officer positions, there are leadership positions available at the district level. Members of the organization can be as involved as they want and are able to take on additional responsibilities according to their interests. After seeing how much was accomplished by Circle Kers after only a few hours of work at the

Spring 2007 DLSSP, I was inspired to become a more active Circle K member.

Through involvement this I began to see how unique Circle K is, especially for a college student organization. Circle K members are some of the friendliest, most enthusiastic, most driven, and most inspiring people… especially considering that we are all just in college. I know that Circle K members will to continue to impact the world, even after graduating from college.

This brings me to my next point: the fellowship aspect of Circle K. Circle K is not just another community service organization. Instead, it is part of a larger group, the Kiwanis Family. The members of Circle K are some of the most amazing and inspiring people I've met and I have a feeling that the friendships made in Circle K will last a lifetime. The amazing people in Circle K make already rewarding service projects into incredibly fun events and the service done to help improve the lives of others takes on a whole new meaning.

Circle K provides opportunities for driven college students to make a difference in the world. When you join Circle K you not only become a member in an organization, but a member of a second family as well.

For more information on Circle K, The Six Cents Initiative, or the Tomorrow Fund,
please visit www.circlek.org..

The Boys and Girls Home

by Kathryn Geiger
Clemson University Circle K

It has been an honor and a pleasure to serve you this past year as your Circle K Governor. During the past 12 months, and more, I have put countless miles on my car, I have spent countless hours of service, and gained countless memories I will hold with me for the rest of my life.

Of all of my travels and memories, a few things specifically about service, leadership and fellowship stand out. I would like to share them with you.

For several years, the Carolinas District of Circle K dedicated its time and money to the Boys and Girls Home at Lake Waccamaw. The Boys and Girls Home is a place for those who have nowhere else to go, a place where forgotten children can take shelter from life for a while until they can learn the lessons they need to take life on.

And Circle K is not alone in its respect and admiration for the Home. Our brothers and sisters in Key Club have been working with them for several years now, and it was actually their passion that ignited ours. Through their example, Circle K realized that working with the Home is something that we have no intention of stopping. We can not, because the stakes for the children there are too high.

This past November, Circle K spent a weekend at the Home. Being there and seeing everyone come together in that place that has taken room in my heart and has left a permanent imprint like few other experiences have. For this particular weekend, we worked on the building that started the Kiwanis Family's relationship with the Home—The Kiwanis Cottage. Seeing the Kiwanis name on the building, on something concrete and lasting, just proved even more to me that what we were doing meant something.

As college students we may not always think that what we are doing is that meaningful, but when you actually take a moment to step back and see the effects of your hard work, you see more than just the effort. You see something that you can take pride in.

For more information on Circle K, The Six Cents Initiative, or the Tomorrow Fund, please visit www.circlek.org..

That weekend, while tearing up carpeting and tacking I saw years of children's feet crossing the old carpeting while learning to walk with a newfound pride in themselves. While sweeping floors, repairing holes in the walls, and painting those walls beside Kiwanis District Secretary Wayne Adams, I saw the decades of a brick and mortar building being the last and best chance children had to become adults. And while walking through the newly painted Kiwanis Cottage with Larry Hewitt and hearing about the further renovations that were planned to provide decades more shelter for children from the outside world, I saw those children being given the opportunity to succeed in life... in some part because of the work we did that weekend. I have come to realize that sometimes in life little things, those small gestures of caring and thought can have a tremendous impact on children and their future.

Now that the Carolinas District of Kiwanis has officially adopted the Boys and Girls Home as a standing district service project, we can finally say that the Kiwanis Family in the Carolinas are united and committed to making the Boys and Girls Home a lasting success. Separate we have all done so much, but together we can do even more.

The second tenet of Circle K is leadership, but as students we are constantly being told that we are the "future" leaders of this country. We're told that "someday" we will affect the lives of those we hope to lead. Constantly we are given a mandate to lead our country into the future, yet we are also told that our time is not now and somehow we'll learn to be effective leaders when the time is right. Thankfully, the Kiwanis Family sees the leadership in all, and it provides its sponsored programs with the tools to be effective leaders now.

For more information on Circle K, The Six Cents Initiative, or the Tomorrow Fund, please visit www.circlek.org.

In Circle K, I went through leadership training courses and applied them to become the best leader I could. I know that if it hadn't been for Circle K, I would not have half the business skills I have today. By going from being a general member to having the chance to serve on the district board for these past two years I have learned how to effectively communicate with a whole array of personalities. I have learned the value of effective time management and organization in juggling a full course load at school and the commitments I have to Circle K.

While these leadership lessons helped in school and Circle K, I did not realize how much of an impact these lessons had in real life until recently. This past summer I saw all these lessons take hold when I started as an intern with a pharmaceutical company and only days after starting I ended up team leader for a group of 12. Going from just an everyday run of the mill summer intern to team leader can be a scary thing at the age of 19. Looking back over the summer, I realized that it was the skills I learned in Circle K that allowed me to be a business leader and do my job effectively. Circle K and the Kiwanis family are helping us become vibrant, effective leaders. Today. Not at some unknown time in the future.

While service and leadership is important, you can't have a whole bunch of college students get together regularly and not expect them to have fun. The fellowship that Circle K offers enables us to impact our world while becoming friends. As a member of Circle K, I have met people from throughout the country and across the globe. I've formed lifelong friendships, created lasting memories, and changed the world for the better. By having a group of people around you who love to do community service as much as you do is a great thing.

For more information on Circle K, The Six Cents Initiative, or the Tomorrow Fund, please visit www.circlek.org..

But aside from fellowship, there is also family. For a lot of college students, myself included, we often find ourselves at schools far away from our families. This can be a very hard, emotional thing for students to deal with at times. If it had not been for Circle K, I probably would not have stayed at Clemson.

My freshman year was very difficult for me. Being 12 hours away from my family, not knowing really any one, and being in a completely different 'culture' was hard for me to adjust to. But then I found Circle K. Almost immediately I felt at home with the other people in the Clemson club. The people I met there inspired me to do more and be more. As I became more involved and realized what Circle K was all about, I discovered I really was not that far from family after all. No matter what predicament the future finds me in, no matter what life provides me or where I am in the world, I know that when I see that sign with a large K that I am home and that I am near family. I'm near all of you—The Kiwanis Family.

(First delivered at Carolinas District of Kiwanis Mid-Year Conference, January 2008).

For more information on Circle K, The Six Cents Initiative, or the Tomorrow Fund, please visit www.circlek.org.

SECTION III:
THIS AND THAT

The final part of this book is a collection of different tidbits, articles and even poems to exemplify the Circle K and Kiwanis Family experience. While the stories and speeches show power coming from the heart, it is arguable that the more brief writings are wisdom coming from the soul. As you read through these writings, it is our hope that you have already made your own commitment to serving your community and that these writings may spark an idea or two in where to start.

For more information on Circle K, The Six Cents Initiative, or the Tomorrow Fund, please visit www.circlek.org..

365 Pieces of Trash

by Dave Kelly

Past Circle K International President (1982-83)

University of Wisconsin-Oshkosh Circle K

As a professional speaker, I get to meet students with all kinds of backgrounds and experiences at a variety of schools located all around the county. One experience that has stayed with me was when I spoke at the U.S. Coast Guard Academy in the fall of 2006.

After a morning training program for the cadets, Victoria Stevens, a 2nd Class Cadet – the equivalent of a college junior – offered to take me on a tour of the campus. As she showed me around, she would occasionally stop to pick up pieces of trash, such as gum wrappers and plastic bottle caps. After a while I asked her if this was part of the Cadet Honor Code and if all of the Cadets were expected to do the same. She told me it wasn't. It was something she just did.

Then she said, "If I pick up at least one piece of trash every day, then that means there are 365 less pieces of garbage in the world."

I was so impressed that I have shared this story with audiences around the country. It is such a perfect example of unselfish service. Cadet Stevens does not have to do what she is doing and, in most cases, it probably goes unnoticed by others. However, she is making a difference in the world.

For many, service can and does become second nature, furthering the development of a lifetime commitment to helping others.

For more information on Circle K, The Six Cents Initiative, or the Tomorrow Fund, please visit www.circlek.org.

For more information on Circle K, The Six Cents Initiative, or the Tomorrow Fund,
please visit www.circlek.org..

Invisible Children

by Kathryn Geiger
Clemson University Circle K

Circle K is all about serving the children of the world so that their lives and communities become a better place. Yet there are so many places that have been left untouched. I realized this when the Clemson Circle K club took on the task of introducing the Invisible Children's Campaign to our campus. Once we heard about the extent of the problem in Uganda we jumped at the chance to bring awareness to the cause. We help a movie showing and a letter writing campaign. Close to 200 people came to the movie and afterwards wrote around 600 letters.

The Invisible Children's Campaign is about bringing aid to the children of Uganda. These children live in a constant state of fear. Fear that is from the knowledge that at any moment they could be forced into captivity by the rebel army and forced to serve as *Children Soldiers*. The children that are captured are forced to kill or be killed, sometimes even killing their own family. They are given drugs and alcohol and are brainwashed against the outside world. Children should never have to live like this. They shouldn't have to walk miles from their homes in the 'bush' to central towns so that they can sleep in drain pipes, allies, parking lots, and bus stations just they have a chance to make it through the night without being taken.

For more information on Circle K, The Six Cents Initiative, or the Tomorrow Fund, please visit www.circlek.org.

Thanks to our movie showing three years ago our campus has taken the campaign and expanded what we can do for the children. Many organizations have taken to holding movie showings but our Student Government also hosts the Gulu Walk, a walk around the outer limits of campus at midnight. The Invisible Children's Campaign has become a staple on our campus. Knowing that I was somehow a part of the beginning of the movement is one of the greatest memories I have, because one small club came together and as a result our entire campus did the same. In some small way I know that we are helping those children and I couldn't ask for anything more.

For more information on Circle K, The Six Cents Initiative, or the Tomorrow Fund, please visit www.circlek.org..

The Book Lady

by Mary Gavalas
Past Kiwanis Governor

The fifth Object of Kiwanis International is: "To provide through Kiwanis clubs, a practical means to form enduring friendships, to render altruistic service, and to build better communities".

Is it really possible to render altruistic service? When I mentor/tutor a child in math, one the teacher has already branded as not able to comprehend or completely unable to do any part of, I spend extra time with him, one on one. I suddenly see a glimmer of light, a very small acceptance, an understanding of the basics in his eyes and a smile on his face. WOW! I feel Great. I am rewarded by knowing that my time has (albeit selfishly) satisfied.

And so it was yet again a few years ago when my home Kiwanis club sponsored a Head Start class. In partnership with our Key Club, one of our major projects was to give the children (3 and 4 year olds) a Christmas party with Santa, a tree, treats and gifts. Our primary gift was a one-on-one hour of reading and then presenting the children with the books we had read to them.

For more information on Circle K, The Six Cents Initiative, or the Tomorrow Fund, please visit www.circlek.org.

All of us left the school feeling WONDERFUL. Altruistic? I do not think so because the reward was immediate. We could sense how the children felt and knew that they had ownership of the books. For many this was the first book they could their own and for others it was the first book in their home.

A couple of weeks later, while ringing the Salvation Army bell at our local Wal-Mart, a small boy came over to me and threw his arms around my waist, yelling, "Mommy, Mommy, It's the book lady!". The mother came over, thanked me for the party and the gift of books for her son. Then she did something very strange. She whispered in my ear, "He loves the books and so do I. But I had to go next door to have someone read them to me so that I could read them to him. So, you see, you helped me, too". Altruistic? What do you think – as the tears rolled down my cheeks?

For more information on Circle K, The Six Cents Initiative, or the Tomorrow Fund, please visit www.circlek.org..

The Summer in Service

by Ali Grotkowski
University of Alberta Circle K

Maybe you'll see me at the Slide
The Giant Kiwanis great fun ride,
Where one dollar tickets are sold
To the excited young and old
Who want to slide.

Maybe I'll be at Heritage days
Putting in time in so many ways
Where countries are visited on a lark
And food is tasted all in one park
And our service pays.

How about catching CKIers all wet?
These people this July truly were set
To wash the bottoms of cars for free
And clean the tops if they could see
The funds that they could get.

For more information on Circle K, The Six Cents Initiative, or the Tomorrow Fund,
please visit www.circlek.org.

Then there's the Masters that is in town

So many countries that did come down

And uniformed people with so many smiles

Volunteer their time after travelling miles

As do some CKI in town.

But more volunteer opportunities lie in wait

Why not go enter the CKI gate

Toward more fun service today

Because it's surely the best way

To volunteer with people who are great!

For more information on Circle K, The Six Cents Initiative, or the Tomorrow Fund, please visit www.circlek.org..

Dandy the Dragon

by Rich Thigpen
Advisor, UCLA Circle K

One of my favorite service projects when I was a Circle K'er at Auburn University was "Dandy the Dragon." Two members would go the East Alabama Medical Center's pediatrics ward, and one would put on a big green dragon costume and the other would act as the interpreter (if Dandy were to speak, the different voices on different days would spoil the illusion for the kids who were in the hospital for lengthy stays). When I was dressed in the Dandy costume, I would usually make a point to visit other rooms around the hospital when I was finished with pediatrics-after all, I figured many older patients who didn't have any local family or friends would appreciate ANY visitor.

On one of these random stops, I went into the room of an elderly man who had tubes hooked up all over his face and body. When he saw me, his pain-ridden face suddenly brightened and he grinned. The nurse attending him said, "My goodness, he's been here for weeks and that's the first time I've seen him smile."

That, to me, demonstrates the purpose of Circle K International: small acts of kindness can brighten the lives of others in ways you can never predict.

For more information on Circle K, The Six Cents Initiative, or the Tomorrow Fund, please visit www.circlek.org.

For more information on Circle K, The Six Cents Initiative, or the Tomorrow Fund,
please visit www.circlek.org..

Behind the Scenes

by Kristina Badali
Kiwanis Club of Verona-Rosedale

The days of planning are finished.
The supplies have been purchased.
The event was held and was a big success.
The clean-up is done.
The after party celebration is scheduled.

Everyone is familiar with those steps above as they are pretty typical of planning a club service project. And we know, whether big or small, the impact of these projects will be great. Many times, we hear about the success stories of Kiwanis Family members helping others outside of our organization. These stories are not only inspirational but continue to motivate us to serve our communities all the more.

For more information on Circle K, The Six Cents Initiative, or the Tomorrow Fund, please visit www.circlek.org.

But what amazes me the most about this organization, and being a Kiwanis Family member, is the impact that serving others has made not only on those we serve but on those of us "behind the scenes." It is during those club meetings/planning stages and social events, in which the magic happens for us. We continue to learn, develop stronger leadership skills, enhance team building skills, learn self confidence, and make life long friends.

Still, there are those who don't realize the value of contributing to our organizations as active members. You know them. The ones who stand in the back of the room too afraid to volunteer, believing they don't have what it takes to be a leader, afraid that they are "different" and that what they have to offer is not as good or important to anyone else. The problem is that they have never been given the encouragement to make a difference, voice their opinion, or even take a stand for what they believe in.

When I was member in Key Club and Circle K, it amazed me how many times I heard, from my peers, that they didn't want to do something because "they were not the best," when I, as well as others, knew that they were capable. All they needed was an "extra push" so they could believe in themselves. For me, this is part of the magic, special feeling, or otherwise known to some as the "Kiwanis Moment" that you get when you are helping others. It is helping others that create the magic of our organization. When our family gets a hold of these types of members, and they see what they are capable of accomplishing. I've been told that it "takes them to another place" where they can feel confident in their selves and their contributions. They are no different from anyone, but unique, special, and can do anything that they put their minds and hearts into.

For more information on Circle K, The Six Cents Initiative, or the Tomorrow Fund, please visit www.circlek.org..

As a Kiwanian and a mentor, through club meetings and activities, I continue to meet those (mostly students) who need an extra push or boost and I will to be there to help. And I know, while they might not ever tell me, that I've made a difference, I see it in their actions and hear it in their words! Through the motivation and mentoring and the support of the Kiwanis family they go away with confidence and courage and can proudly state, "I am the best" and "I can do it".

It gives me great pride to be a current and past member of the Kiwanis Family organization. Organizations that in addition to helping our others help our membership grow and make an impact on the world. The next time you volunteer at a service project, take a minute to think about the people "behind the scenes." There's a good chance that there is someone there who once needed the same support, guidance and encouragement that they are giving.

For more information on Circle K, The Six Cents Initiative, or the Tomorrow Fund, please visit www.circlek.org.

For more information on Circle K, The Six Cents Initiative, or the Tomorrow Fund,
please visit www.circlek.org..

www.ingramcontent.com/pod-product-compliance
Lightning Source LLC
Chambersburg PA
CBHW060759050426
42449CB00008B/1450